To our precious daughter on
Christmas, 2015
Sent with all our love!
Bon Appetit!
Mum + Dad
x x x

A BIRD IN THE HAND

DIANA HENRY

A BIRD IN THE HAND

chicken recipes for every day and every mood

MITCHELL BEAZLEY

An Hachette UK Company

www.hachette.co.uk

First published in Great Britain in 2015
by Mitchell Beazley, a division of Octopus
Publishing Group Ltd
Endeavour House, 189 Shaftesbury Avenue
London WC2H 8JY

www.octopusbooks.co.uk

Diana Henry asserts her moral right to be identified
as the author of this work.

ISBN 978 1 84533 896 1

A CIP catalogue record for this book is available
from the British Library.

Printed and bound in China

10 9 8 7 6 5 4 3 2

Publisher: Denise Bates
Art Director: Jonathan Christie
Photographer: Laura Edwards
Design and Art Direction: Miranda Harvey
Editor: Lucy Bannell
Home Economist and Food Stylist: Joss Herd
Senior Production Manager: Katherine Hockley

contents

introduction 6

suppers: dishes for every night of the week 8

the spice route: scented, perfumed, hot 48

the main attraction: Sunday lunches and posh dinners 72

chooks, shoots and leaves: chicken salads 108

feast: let's celebrate 132

summer and smoke: griddled and barbecued 154

pure comfort: dishes to warm and soothe 174

remains of the day: what to do with the rest of that bird... 200

index 221

introduction

Chicken, in its many guises, has always been part of my life. Chicken Maryland, a big chunk of golden-skinned bird served with fried bananas and bacon, was what my siblings and I ordered when we went out to supper as kids. Sitting on modish chairs with scratchy seats, our feet barely touching the ground, we tackled plates of this in the local 'grillroom' (such things existed in the 1970s) with appetites that were bigger than our child-sized bellies. At home, roast chicken with parsley and onion stuffing – served with my mum's chips – was the meal that always provoked cheers. As teenagers, picnics weren't based on sandwiches, but on a whole cold roast chicken whose meat we would tear apart and stuff into soft white rolls. Chicken curry (the old-fashioned British kind made with curry paste, raisins and the remains of the roast) was the exotic accompaniment to Sunday night telly. When I was taken to supper by a boy I really fancied – only to have him tell me that he was interested in my best friend – I was eating chicken (it was probably the only time in my life I didn't polish it off). And the first meal I ever cooked for my partner – at his request – was a braise of chicken, leeks and apples (the recipe is on page 192).

Chicken is the thing I sneak into the fridge to steal (usually with a bottle of HP sauce nearby) and the first dish I order when I arrive in Portugal (piri piri) or the States (fried). At the end of a filming day with Hugh Fearnley-Whittingstall (I was a TV producer before I was a food writer), we were finishing dinner when Hugh FW looked at the remains of the bird on my plate. It was hard to tell from the clean little bones what I had eaten, but Hugh knew. 'What did you do to that chicken?' he asked (with more than a little admiration). 'I stripped it to its bones,' I said. 'Just as I was taught.' This is down to my dad, who always pointed out the little morsels you hadn't managed to extricate from the carcass and was fond of all the tastiest bits: the oysters (those little plump cushions of meat on the underside), the crisp tipped wings, the juicy thighs. In my family we were instructed in the enjoyment of chicken.

And it appears to be dear – or at least a good buddy – to others, too. Fried chicken, chicken tikka masala, jerk chicken, many cultures have cherished chicken dishes. It is also the meat most people – even those who aren't keen on meat – will eat. It's amenable, too, and I mean that in a good way. It's the basic outfit that you can dress down (for picky children) or dress up (on those occasions when you want to present a dish that prompts everyone to ask for the recipe). My efforts with it range from bashing strips of chicken breast, dipping them in egg and breadcrumbs and frying them (a favourite of my kids), to brining a big expensive bird and serving it on a platter surrounded by glossy chestnuts and prunes (for the Christmas meal). In between, I make chicken dishes from all over the world. There isn't a week goes by that I don't cook chicken at least once.

Over the years, I've opted to buy more expensive chicken but less often; a roast chicken is just the beginning of many meals as you have stock and leftover flesh, making even a pricier bird a relatively economical option. I buy a mixture of free-range and Freedom Food birds. Freedom Food poultry is reared to the RSPCA's welfare standards and costs only a little more than intensively reared poultry, so it's hard to justify not buying it. I'm lucky that my butcher stocks chickens from two great farms as well: Sutton Hoo and – my favourite – Fosse Meadows. There are other more expensive birds, from Label Anglais all the way to Bresse chicken (Bresse is very expensive but a great treat if you're a chicken lover). The Fosse Meadows bird does have a much better flavour than Freedom Food chicken and, when I want a golden, crisp-skinned roast, this is what I splash out on. But you can, with good ideas and careful cooking, turn less expensive chicken into a fantastic meal. When 'foodies' complain about how 'tasteless' they find regular chicken, I'm really not sure what they're doing to it. How should you shop for chicken? Simply buy the best you can.

Readers and friends often ask for help with chicken. How can they make it different, what can they do that isn't the same old, same old? Even though my job is to think about food, I often have the same problem myself when I start to wonder about the evening meal. So I gathered up all the dishes I could – old favourites and new ones, mostly nothing too difficult – to put in this book. There are also short pieces of writing on braising and roasting that you should read, but I've tried to keep instructions on method to a minimum. Cooking chicken is basically easy and there's no reason to complicate it. I just wanted to give you as many recipes and new ideas as possible. Many of the obvious classics are missing; other people have given recipes for Thai green chicken curry, so you hardly need that again. Instead, I've tried to offer the less well-known and riffs on the familiar. The book could have been three times the size, but sometimes less is more and I thought it was better to have a useful book in the kitchen than a thick, comprehensive tome.

All the recipes in here are now part of my repertoire. I hope they become part of yours, too, and that the evenings when you look at the packet of chicken thighs in your fridge and think, 'What the hell am I going to do with those?' are a thing of the past. If you have chicken in the fridge, a good meal is never far away.

suppers *dishes for every night of the week*

spanish supper: chicken, morcilla and sherry

Simple chicken thighs transformed into something special. If you can't get morcilla (Spanish black pudding), use British black pudding instead. The cream isn't at all mandatory, I often leave it out, it just depends on your mood (sometimes you want a treat and a bit of luxury). Increase the quantities and you have an excellent supper for friends for very little effort.

SERVES 2

1 tbsp olive oil
salt and pepper
4 skin-on bone-in chicken thighs
8 slices of morcilla, or black pudding
½ large onion, cut into slim crescent moon-shaped wedges
200ml (7fl oz) dry sherry, plus 3½ tbsp more if needed
3½ tbsp double cream
1 tbsp toasted pine nuts
1 tbsp chopped flat-leaf parsley leaves

Preheat the oven to 180°C/350°F/gas mark 4.

Heat the oil in a small ovenproof frying pan that can fit the thighs and morcilla snugly in a single layer. Season the chicken and brown on both sides just for colour, not to cook it through. Take out of the pan and set aside. Add the morcilla to the pan and cook it lightly on both sides, then remove it, too, and set aside with the chicken. If there's a lot of fat in the pan, pour all but 1 tbsp of it off. Don't wash the pan or try to dislodge any bits stuck to it; there's flavour there.

Add the onion to the pan and colour it lightly; you don't need it to soften. Deglaze the pan with the sherry, scraping the base with a wooden spoon to remove all the flavoursome scraps, then return the chicken and morcilla. Bake in the hot oven for 40 minutes; if you stick the tip of a sharp knife into the underside of one of the thighs, the juices that run out should be clear with no trace of pink; if the chicken is not quite ready, cook for a few minutes more, then test again.

There should still be sherry left in the pan, now mixed with the cooking juices. If there isn't, and the pan is quite dry, add 3½ tbsp more and stir it into the rest. Put the pan over a medium heat (be sure to hold the handle with a tea towel or an oven glove) and pour in the cream, heating it until it bubbles. Sprinkle with the pine nuts and parsley and serve immediately.

mexican chicken and pumpkin with pepita pesto

Use a big roasting tin to cook this – an old bashed one is great – and take it to the table. This is casual eating at its very best, so I don't bother to transfer the food to a platter. Quinoa and a big salad of Romaine leaves and avocado are great on the side.

The pepita pesto – stir the crumbled feta into it rather than sprinkling it on top if you prefer – is good with plain roast or griddled chicken as well.

SERVES 4

FOR THE CHICKEN AND PUMPKIN

8 skin-on bone-in chicken
   joints or thighs
1 tbsp soft light brown sugar
leaves from 4 sprigs of thyme
3 tsp dried oregano
2 tsp ground cumin
2 tsp ground allspice
6 tbsp olive oil
juice of 1 lime
juice of ½ orange
salt and pepper
900g (2lb) well-flavoured
   pumpkin, peeled, deseeded
   and cut into thick wedges
60g (2oz) feta cheese, finely
   crumbled, to serve

FOR THE PESTO

20g (¾oz) pumpkin seeds
60g (2oz) sprigs of coriander,
   plus more to serve
20g (¾oz) cashew nuts
2 garlic cloves, chopped
juice of 1½ limes
125ml (4fl oz) extra virgin
   olive oil
1 red chilli, halved, deseeded
   and finely chopped, plus
   more to serve (optional)

Put the chicken in a shallow dish. Mix together the sugar, thyme, oregano, spices, 4 tbsp of the regular oil, both the citrus juices and salt and pepper and pour this marinade over the chicken. Turn the chicken round to coat well, then cover and marinate in the fridge for a couple of hours. Bring it to room temperature before you cook it.

For the pesto, put the pumpkin seeds in a dry frying pan and place over a medium heat. Stir for a couple of minutes, or until they turn a shade darker and smell a little toasted (this method also works for spice seeds and nuts). Put in a food processor with all the other ingredients except the chilli. Blend to a rough purée. Scrape into a bowl, stir in the chilli and set aside until you want to use it.

When ready to cook, preheat the oven to 180°C/350°F/gas mark 4. Transfer the chicken, skin side up, to a roasting tin or a large, broad, shallow ovenproof dish. Dot the pumpkin wedges around the chicken. Brush the pumpkin with the remaining 2 tbsp of regular oil and season. Put into the hot oven and cook for 40 minutes, basting every so often.

Check the flesh of the chicken to see whether it's cooked or not: if you stick the tip of a sharp knife into the underside of a thick joint, the juice that runs out should be clear with no trace of pink. Serve with some pesto spooned over (offer the rest on the side) and scatter with crumbled feta and sprigs of coriander and some more chilli, if you want.

saltimbocca

Classics are classics for a reason: they're great dishes. This is usually made with veal, but you can also make it with chicken breasts. An excellent dish for when there are just two of you. It's quickly made and a bit of a treat. Because of the gentle cooking, the Parma ham stays fairly soft. Supper on a plate in 10 minutes.

SERVES 2

2 skinless boneless chicken breasts (not too large)
salt and pepper
2 slices of Parma ham
2 sage leaves
about ½ tbsp plain flour
2 tsp olive oil
15g (½oz) unsalted butter
200ml (7fl oz) dry Marsala

Put each breast between two pieces of greaseproof paper and, using a rolling pin, bash them to a thickness of about 5mm (¼in), but don't bash so hard that they break up. Season. Wrap a slice of Parma ham round each chicken escalope and put a sage leaf on top. Some people secure the ham and sage with a cocktail stick but, once you have dusted the chicken in flour and fried it, the sage does stay in place. Lightly dust the escalopes on both sides with the flour.

Heat the oil and butter in a large frying pan. Cook the chicken over a medium heat for about three and a half minutes on each side. Check the flesh of the chicken to see whether it's cooked or not: if you stick the tip of a sharp knife into a breast, the juice that runs out should be clear with no trace of pink. Remove and keep warm.

Add the Marsala to the pan and bubble it away over a high heat until thickened and reduced by about half. Taste for seasoning and serve poured over the chicken. Rosemary- or thyme-flavoured potatoes, either sautéed or roasted with olive oil, are lovely on the side, as are some simple greens.

baked chicken with tarragon and dijon mustard

Great for a midweek supper. It's a kind of hassle-free chicken with tarragon.

SERVES 4–6

8 tbsp Dijon mustard
chopped leaves from 6 sprigs of tarragon
50g (1¾oz) unsalted butter, softened
8 skinless bone-in chicken joints
salt and pepper
25g (scant 1oz) breadcrumbs (from stale, not fresh bread)

Preheat the oven to 220°C/425°F/gas mark 7. Mash the Dijon mustard with the tarragon and butter until it is well mixed together. Put the chicken into a roasting tin (or ovenproof serving dish) and brush or spoon on the mustard mixture. Season, then press on the breadcrumbs.

Roast in the hot oven for 35 minutes. The chicken should be cooked through. Check this by piercing the flesh near the bone, with the tip of a sharp knife, in one of the larger joints. The juices should run clear with no trace of pink. If not, cook for a few minutes more then test again. The top should be a lovely golden colour.

Serve immediately with the cooking juices that have gathered round the chicken, some boiled waxy potatoes and a green salad or green beans.

cumin and turmeric roast chicken with smashed avocado and corn cakes

A good and quick supper. If you want to keep things really simple, don't bother with the corn cakes: brown rice is fine on the side. Roast peppers or roast tomatoes would be good too, as their sweetness works well against the spices in the chicken. Be careful about seasoning the avocado and adding the sherry vinegar. You mustn't overdo it, but at the same time this part of the dish is not supposed to be bland, it needs a bit of kick.

SERVES 4

FOR THE CORN CAKES

50g (1¾oz) fine cornmeal or
    polenta
50g (1¾oz) plain flour
250g (9oz) sweetcorn
3 large eggs, lightly beaten
75ml (2½fl oz) milk
40g (1½oz) unsalted butter,
    melted and cooled
1 red and 1 green chilli,
    deseeded and finely sliced
2 spring onions, chopped
salt and pepper
groundnut oil, to fry

FOR THE CHICKEN

3 tsp turmeric
3 tsp hot paprika
2 tsp ground cumin
2 tbsp olive oil
1½ tsp soft light brown sugar
35g (1¼oz) unsalted butter
3 tsp English mustard
8 skin-on chicken joints

FOR THE AVOCADO

2 ripe avocados
6 tsp sherry vinegar
juice of 1 lime
4 tbsp double cream
3 tbsp chopped coriander

You can make the corn cake batter well in advance. Simply put the first six ingredients into a food processor and, using the pulse button so the corn gets chopped rather than puréed, mix everything together. Stir in the chillies and spring onions and season to taste. Set aside.

Preheat the oven to 190°C/375°F/gas mark 5. For the chicken, mix the spices, olive oil, sugar, butter and mustard together with some seasoning. Season the joints, then spread the spice paste all over. Put the chicken in a roasting tin and cook in the hot oven for 40 minutes. Baste every so often with the cooking juices. It is cooked when the juices in the thickest part run clear, with no trace of pink.

Meanwhile, halve the avocados and remove the stones. Scoop out the flesh and put it in a bowl. Crush it very roughly with a fork or pestle, but don't mash it. It should still have some structure. Gently stir in the other ingredients. They shouldn't completely blend together, that way you meet contrasting flavours as you eat it.

Just before you're going to serve the chicken, heat some groundnut oil in a frying pan and, once it's hot, spoon dollops of the corn cake batter into the pan (about 7.5cm/3in across is a good size). Once each cake has set underneath, flip it over and cook until golden on the other side.

Serve the corn cakes and smashed avocado with the chicken.

chicken with prunes in red wine

This is inspired by the food of south west France, but it isn't cooked in a traditional way. I've made it into one of those dishes that, thankfully, looks after itself; it's a very easy version of a classic. You can have it on the table in 40 minutes. Pretty good for a dish that has such depth.

SERVES 4

FOR THE CHICKEN

8 skin-on bone-in chicken thighs, or a mixture of joints
2 large onions, halved
1 tbsp olive oil
salt and pepper
300ml (½ pint) red wine
16 mi-cuit prunes, or soft good-quality prunes
2 garlic cloves, finely chopped
½ tbsp crème de cassis (optional)

FOR THE HERB CRUST

good handful of flat-leaf parsley leaves, finely chopped
salt flakes
2 garlic cloves, finely chopped
2 tbsp coarse breadcrumbs (I prefer whole grain bread here)
1½ tbsp olive oil
2 tbsp brandy or Armagnac

Preheat the oven to 190°C/375°F/gas mark 5. Trim the skin on the chicken so it just covers them (you just want to get rid of those straggly bits). Slice each onion half into large half-moon shaped wedges (about 1.5cm/¾in thick at their thickest). Heat the oil in an ovenproof dish that can hold all the chicken in a single layer. Season the chicken and brown it on all sides over a medium-high heat, just to colour it, not cook it through. Remove the chicken and pour away all but 1 tbsp of fat. Add the onions and cook for about four minutes, season and return the chicken, skin side up. Make sure both chicken and the onions are quite moist with fat. Put into the oven for 20 minutes.

Heat the wine in a small pan and add the prunes. Simmer for two minutes, then add the garlic and the cassis (if using; I just like the extra fruity taste it imparts), then set aside.

To make the herb crust, put the parsley, salt flakes (and some pepper) and the garlic into a mortar and pestle and pound together. Or just chop the parsley and garlic finely and season. In either case, mix to a rough paste with the breadcrumbs and olive oil, then add the brandy.

When the chicken has cooked for 20 minutes, turn the onions to colour on the other side, dot the prunes among them and pour in the wine. Cook for 10 minutes, then spread the herb paste over the chicken. Cook for another 10 minutes. The wine should be reduced and the prunes plump.

thai chicken burgers with asian slaw

I usually serve these fairly plainly, simply griddled with the slaw on the side, but you can put the burgers into sesame buns with ginger mayo. For the mayo I just use good bought stuff mixed with some fromage frais and add crushed garlic, lime juice, a little grated root ginger and plenty of chopped pickled ginger.

SERVES 6

FOR THE BURGERS

500g (1lb 2oz) minced chicken

100g (3½oz) fresh white
    breadcrumbs

1 lemon grass stalk

1 small onion, finely chopped

3 garlic cloves, grated

2cm (¾in) root ginger, grated

finely grated zest of 1 lime

1 tbsp fish sauce

2 tbsp chopped coriander

2 tsp caster sugar

a little oil (olive, rapeseed or
    groundnut), to brush

brown rice, or butter, soft rolls,
    mayonnaise and chilli sauce,
    to serve

FOR THE SLAW

¼ red cabbage

¼ white or Savoy cabbage

300g (10½oz) carrots, peeled
    and cut into matchsticks

10 radishes, sliced wafer thin
    (a mandoline is best here)

handful of mint leaves

handful of basil leaves

handful of coriander leaves

1 tbsp fish sauce

2 tbsp lime juice

1 tbsp rice vinegar

1 tbsp caster sugar

1 red chilli, halved, deseeded
    and cut into slivers

Put the chicken and breadcrumbs into a bowl. Remove the coarse outer layers from the lemon grass and trim the top and base. Chop the rest – the softer bit of the lemon grass – as finely as you can. Add this to the chicken with the onion, garlic, ginger, lime zest, fish sauce, coriander and sugar. Mix everything together well with your hands (it really is the best way to incorporate it all). Shape into six patties and put them on a baking sheet. Cover with cling film and refrigerate for about 30 minutes to allow them to firm up a little.

Remove and discard the coarse central core from each of the cabbages and shred the leaves finely. Put into a bowl with the carrots, radishes and herbs. Make the dressing by mixing the fish sauce, lime juice and rice vinegar together in a cup with the caster sugar; whisk to encourage the sugar to dissolve. Add the chilli. Throw this over the vegetables in the bowl.

Heat a griddle pan and brush the burgers on each side with a little oil. (You can also fry the burgers, just heat the oil in a frying pan instead.) Cook the burgers over a medium heat at first, then over a lower heat once they're coloured, for five minutes on each side. Take a peek into the middle of one (use the point of a sharp knife) to check that the chicken is cooked all the way through, with no trace of pink.

Serve the burgers with the slaw, either with brown rice on the side (the healthy option) or in lightly buttered buns with mayonnaise or your favourite chilli sauce (or both). I like them in a bun with mayo, chopped pickled chilli and pickled ginger.

roast chicken, garlic and potatoes in the pan with watercress, cashel blue and walnut butter

This is one of the easiest suppers I cook and one of my favourite weeknight meals. Sometimes I add mushrooms, Jerusalem artichokes (scrub them well and halve them lengthways), or wedges of onion. The important thing is to make sure there is room for everything in the pan you are using, as you need the chicken to lie in a single layer so that it becomes brown and crispy, it shouldn't 'sweat'.

You don't have to use Cashel Blue cheese – I just really like it – you could use Gorgonzola or another blue. And of course other flavoured butters – thyme and Parmesan, mustard, or chilli and coriander – would be good, too.

SERVES 4

FOR THE CHICKEN
550g (1lb 4oz) waxy baby
    potatoes (no need to peel)
8 mixed skin-on bone-in
    chicken joints, or thighs
2 bulbs of garlic, separated
    into cloves but not peeled
salt and pepper
6 tbsp extra virgin olive oil
1 tbsp balsamic vinegar
sea salt flakes

FOR THE BUTTER
75g (2¾oz) unsalted butter,
    at room temperature
25g (scant 1oz) finely chopped
    watercress leaves
40g (1½oz) Cashel blue cheese,
    crumbled
25g (scant 1oz) walnuts,
    roughly chopped

Preheat the oven to 200°C/400°F/gas mark 6.

Halve the potatoes unless they are really small. Trim the chicken joints of any scraggy bits of skin or fat to make them neat. Put the potatoes and the garlic into a big shallow ovenproof dish (I use a shallow cast-iron pan that measures 30cm/12in across). It has to be big enough to take the chicken in a single layer; you don't want the joints to be piled on top of each other or they won't crisp and brown properly. Add the joints, season and pour over the oil and balsamic. Toss with your hands to coat everything in a little oil then arrange so the chicken pieces are lying skin side up. Season the chicken with sea salt so that it crisps the skin and roast for 40–45 minutes in the hot oven. You need to move the potatoes around a little halfway through cooking, so they don't get more colour on one side than the other.

Meanwhile, prepare the butter. Either pound the butter in a mortar and pestle, or beat in a small bowl with a wooden spoon, with all the other ingredients. Once everything is mixed together, put it in the fridge to firm up, then mold it into a sausage shape, wrap in cling film or greaseproof paper and return it to the fridge until you need it.

Serve the chicken and potatoes in the dish in which they were cooked with rounds of the butter melting over the top. A green salad or roast onions would be good on the side. And actually pickled pears (or pear chutney) are rather good with this, too.

vietnamese lemon grass and chilli chicken

I sometimes think I could live on Vietnamese food. I love the key flavours and I adore the balance of hot, sour, salty and sweet that is such a dominant characteristic. This is incredibly easy, somewhere between a stir-fry and a sauté, with just enough sauce to coat the pieces of chicken.

SERVES 4

800g (1lb 12oz) skinless boneless chicken thighs, or mini fillets
2 lemon grass stalks
4 tbsp fish sauce
2½ tbsp caster sugar, to taste
2 red chillies, halved, deseeded and shredded
4 garlic cloves, crushed
2 tbsp groundnut or sunflower oil (or other oil of your choice)
1 onion, halved, cut into slim crescent moon-shaped slices
125ml (4fl oz) chicken stock
juice of ½–1 lime, plus more if needed
2 tbsp sprigs of purple amaranth, or coriander (optional)
½ tbsp sesame seeds, to serve (optional)

Trim any fat from the thighs and cut the flesh into bite-sized pieces. Remove the coarse outer layers from the lemon grass and trim the top and base. Chop the rest – the softer bit of the lemon grass – as finely as you can. Put half of this into a bowl with the fish sauce, caster sugar, half the chillies, all the garlic and the chopped chicken. Mix together with your hands, cover with cling film and put into the fridge. Leave to marinate for at least four hours; overnight is even better. Bring it to room temperature before cooking.

Heat the oil in a wide-based saucepan or a wok set over a medium heat. Add the chicken and cook on all sides, getting a really good colour all over it. Add the reserved chillies, reserved lemon grass and the onion and stir-fry until the onion starts to soften. Be careful not to burn the chillies or the lemon grass. Pour in the stock, then reduce the heat, cover and allow the chicken to cook for about five minutes.

Remove the lid, increase the heat and continue to cook until the liquid is reduced. You want a mixture that is wetter than a stir-fry but drier than a braise. Add lime juice to taste, then check for seasoning and sweet-sour balance, adjusting with sugar and lime. Sprinkle with the amaranth leaves or coriander and sesame seeds, if you like, and serve with brown rice and stir-fried greens.

kachin chicken curry

This is adapted from one of my favourite books, Burma: Rivers of Flavor, *by Naomi Duguid. It's full of recipes that are healthy, fresh, light and unexpected. This dish is pretty mild, so I like it with the Chilli sauce on page 57 to lift it all.*

SERVES 4

700g (1lb 9oz) skinless bone-in chicken thighs
6 garlic cloves, finely chopped
2.5cm (1in) root ginger, peeled and grated
1 tsp sea salt flakes
4 small dried red chillies, finely chopped
1½ tsp ground coriander
½ tsp turmeric
1 tbsp groundnut oil
salt and pepper
3 spring onions, chopped
1 tbsp chopped coriander leaves
lime wedges

Halve each chicken thigh by chopping through the centre, cutting right through the bone; you can cut each thigh in four if you want, it does cook more quickly that way. (You need a meat cleaver or a heavy knife for this.) Be careful that there are no splinters of bone in the chicken flesh.

Pound together the garlic, ginger, salt, chillies, ground coriander and turmeric in a mortar and pestle until you have something like a paste. Add 1 tbsp of water, put the chicken in a bowl and pour the paste over it. Turn the chicken over to make sure it all gets coated. If you have time, cover it and put it in the fridge for an hour or so. Bring it to room temperature before cooking.

Add 2 tbsp more water and the groundnut oil to the chicken, then put everything – including the marinade juices – in a wide heavy-based pan that has a tight-fitting lid. Place over a medium-low heat, cover and bring to a simmer. Reduce the heat to very low and cook for 45 minutes. That sounds like a long time, but it should be slow and gentle. Taste for seasoning and adjust it if necessary. Top with the spring onions and chopped coriander, plus the chilli sauce suggested in the recipe introduction (if you feel like it) and lime wedges. Rice topped with crispy-fried shallots (see page 220) is good on the side, as is a vibrant, crunchy salad.

puerto rican chicken and rice

A pretty lazy dish – because you just leave everything to cook – and a good one to make midweek or on a Friday night. It's really important to rinse the rice before cooking it. Achiote paste is a blend of ground annatto seeds, cumin, allspice and oregano and can be found online (from www.souschef. co.uk and also www.coolchile.co.uk). It's pretty essential as it has a unique taste and the annatto imparts an incredible yellow-orange colour. You do need fresh tomato sauce, not ketchup.

SERVES 4–6

FOR THE MARINADE
coarsely ground black pepper
2 garlic cloves, crushed
1½ tsp dried oregano
2 tbsp olive oil
juice of 2 limes

FOR THE REST
1 chicken, jointed into 8,
   or bone-in thighs and
   drumsticks
3 tbsp olive oil
salt and pepper
75g (2¾oz) ham, or raw pork
   belly, or bacon, in chunks
1 onion, roughly chopped
1 red pepper, sliced
1 green pepper, sliced
2 garlic cloves, finely chopped
6 allspice berries
1 tbsp achiote paste
2 red chillies, sliced into rings
6 tbsp home-made (see page
   153) or bought tomato sauce
568ml (1 pint) chicken stock
170g (6oz) basmati rice,
   washed well
3 sprigs of thyme
2 bay leaves
100g (3½oz) green olives
   stuffed with pimento
1 tbsp capers, rinsed
lime wedges, to serve

Make the marinade in a dish in which the chicken will fit by just mixing everything together. Add the chicken and turn it over so it gets coated properly. Cover with cling film and put in the fridge for a couple of hours. When ready to cook, preheat the oven to 190°C/375°F/gas mark 5.

Heat the oil in a broad shallow pan, season the chicken and brown the pieces all over, in batches if necessary so as not to overcrowd the pan. (You want to colour it well, not cook it through.) Take the chicken out of the pan and set it aside. Add the ham (or pork or bacon) to the pan and brown it all over, lift out with a slotted spoon and add to the chicken. Put the onion and peppers into the same pan and sauté over a medium heat until the peppers are softening. Stir in the garlic, allspice, achiote paste and chillies and cook for another two minutes, stirring. Add the tomato sauce and stir this in, too. The achiote paste should dissolve. Heat up the chicken stock.

If you are cooking in a really big shallow pan, or paella pan, you can continue in this. Many people don't have a pan big enough to accommodate all the chicken in a single layer and still have room for the rice, so transfer the chicken (including any juices), ham and vegetables a to a big, wide ovenproof dish (the one I use for this is 30cm/12in in diameter). Pour the rice all round the chicken, pour over the stock, add the thyme and bay leaves and season everything really well.

Put in the preheated oven and cook for 40 minutes, until all the stock has been absorbed and the top is golden. You don't need to stir the rice or cover it or do anything with the dish as it cooks (in fact it's important not to stir it). Scatter on the olives and capers about 15 minutes before the end of the cooking time. Serve with lime wedges.

bourbon and marmalade-glazed drumsticks

This is lovely with a salad that cuts through the sweetness – watercress and shaved fennel is good – with a buttermilk dressing. Brown rice or spelt are perfect alongside.

SERVES 4

8 drumsticks
150g (5½oz) orange marmalade
4 tsp Dijon mustard
3 tbsp bourbon
2 garlic cloves, crushed
2 red chillies, halved, deseeded and finely chopped
2 oranges (preferably thin-skinned), halved and cut into wedges (about 2cm/¾in thick)
salt and pepper

Make small slits in the drumsticks with a sharp knife. In a small bowl, mix 2 tbsp of the marmalade and 1 tsp of the mustard. Set aside. In another bowl, mix the remaining marmalade – squash it down with the back of spoon to break it up – the remaining mustard, the bourbon, garlic and chillies. Put the chicken into this and turn it over so it gets well coated. Cover and put in the fridge for a few hours (or leave it all day, or overnight if you prefer). Bring it to room temperature before cooking.

When you're ready to cook, preheat the oven to 210°C/410°F/gas mark 6½. Put the drumsticks – with all the marinade and any juices – into a roasting tin or gratin dish where they can lie in a single layer. Add the orange wedges. Turn the chicken and oranges over so that the oranges get coated in the marinade, too. Season everything with salt and pepper.

Roast for 40–45 minutes, until the drumsticks are cooked through, glossy and almost caramelized. In the last 10 minutes of the cooking time, brush the top of the drumsticks with the reserved marmalade and mustard.

Lift the oranges and drumsticks on to a serving platter and spoon some of the juices over the top. You can't eat the orange skin, but the flesh is nice: sweet and tart.

hot italian chicken with peppers and chilli

Couldn't be simpler… and yet this dish packs a punch. Try to resist adding onions, tomatoes or any other ingredients or flavourings: this is good because it's simple. It is based on a Calabrian recipe.

SERVES 4–6

2 tbsp olive oil
salt and pepper
1 chicken, skin-on, jointed into 8
5 red (or red and yellow) peppers
4 garlic cloves, finely sliced
3 tsp chilli flakes
35ml (1fl oz) red wine vinegar
2 tbsp balsamic vinegar
6 sprigs of oregano

Preheat the oven to 190°C/375°F/gas mark 5.

Heat the oil in an ovenproof sauté pan or shallow casserole. Season the chicken and brown it in the oil on both sides. It should be lovely and golden. Remove and set aside once it's well coloured. Tip all but 2 tbsp of fat out of the pan, but don't clean it.

Halve, core and deseed the peppers and cut the flesh into strips about 1cm (½in) wide. Heat the fat in the pan and fry the peppers until they are slightly singed and beginning to soften. Season and add the garlic and chilli and cook for another two minutes. Deglaze the pan with the vinegars and stir everything around. Add the leaves of two of the sprigs of oregano, then return the chicken (with any juices that have run out) to the pan on top of the peppers (the peppers should be mostly covered by the chicken and the chicken should be lying in a single layer, skin side up). Scatter on the rest of the oregano.

Put into the hot oven and cook, uncovered, for 40 minutes. The chicken should be cooked: check by piercing the flesh of one of the legs, with the tip of a sharp knife, at the thickest part near the bone. The juices should run clear with no trace of pink. If you find that the chicken is getting too dark on top during cooking, then cover with foil.

Serve immediately with potatoes you've fried or roasted in olive oil and a green salad.

casa lucio's chicken with garlic

Casa Lucio is a Madrid institution. The great and the good dine here – everyone from the royal family to Spanish movie stars and footballers – and well heeled Madrileños, too. It isn't cheap but the food is simple, old-fashioned and good.

This is not a grand dish at all, but one of the quickest and most satisfying in the book. You have to pay attention to it while you're cooking – turning the chicken and altering the heat from time to time – but it doesn't take great skill. I finish the dish with dry sherry rather than white wine and leave the saffron as optional (it's a very good recipe without it).

Lots of different accompaniments work here. Serve it with sautéed or olive oil-roast potatoes and a green salad; roast tomatoes and rice cooked with saffron; or baby spinach leaves and rice tossed with chunks of fried chorizo.

You do need either a meat cleaver or a heavy knife to chop the chicken thighs. Frying chicken thighs that are cut into pieces, but retain the bone, is common in Spanish cooking.

SERVES 4

8 skinless bone-in chicken thighs
salt and pepper
1 bulb of garlic, plus 2 garlic cloves, finely chopped
olive oil
1 tsp sherry vinegar
4 tbsp dry sherry
a few saffron strands (optional)
handful of chopped flat-leaf parsley leaves (optional)

Using a meat cleaver or a good heavy knife, cut the thighs into 5cm (2in) pieces, then check to make sure there aren't any little splinters of bone left. Sprinkle with salt and leave for 10 minutes.

Separate the cloves in the bulb of garlic but don't peel them. Bash each one with the side of a broad-bladed knife to slightly crush.

Heat about 1cm (½in) of olive oil in a large frying pan until very hot. Add the chicken and whole garlic cloves and cook over a high heat, shaking and moving the pieces around for about four minutes until they have a good colour, then reduce the heat a little and continue to cook, turning the chicken, for about another 10 minutes, or until cooked through. Drain in a large sieve, getting rid of the oil.

Add the chopped garlic, vinegar, sherry, saffron (if using) and some salt and pepper to the pan. Bring to the boil, return the chicken pieces and toss until the chicken is glossy and the liquid has been absorbed. Everyone (or at least the food fashionable) seems to think it's very passé to scatter dishes with parsley these days, but do it if you want to.

chicken loves booze

You know the scenario. You're home late. You're tired and fed up. You could murder a packet of crisps and a gin and tonic (and consider pouring yourself a glass, even though the tonic is flat). This is the kind of night when you need a treat. Self-control has no place here. The key thing, though, is to give yourself a treat worth having: a slightly luxurious meal, but one you can make quickly.

For such emergencies it's useful to have these: a bottle each of vermouth, dry Marsala, cider, sherry and Calvados. They're all good for transforming simple ingredients quickly. If you've bought a chicken breast or a packet of thighs on the way home, a bit of booze will help you make something of them. The possibilities are mostly old-fashioned – the classics of bistros and trattorias – but they're none the worse for that.

One of the great things about chicken is its adaptability. It can take herby, fruity, sweet and savoury accompaniments, so you can improvise according to what you have. Bash a chicken breast first between two sheets of greaseproof paper with a rolling pin, to make an escalope. Gently sauté it in butter. Deglaze the pan with either vermouth, dry Marsala or Calvados. Whichever alcohol you use, slosh it in, let it bubble and reduce over a high heat, then lower the heat and add cream. You can also throw in an appropriate herb – tarragon and chervil work with vermouth, thyme with Calvados – or cook something else in the pan, too. Mushrooms are brilliant with Marsala, for example: take the chicken out, sauté the mushrooms really briskly, then add the Marsala and cream and return the chicken to heat through. Or sauté wedges of peeled apple if you're using Calvados.

The only rule with alcohol is to boil it, otherwise it tastes 'raw' and you need the booze to combine with the rest of the dish. Braises – such as coq au vin – require more alcohol (and usually stock, too, as they're cooked in more liquid) and it's less potent (wine or cider rather than spirits or fortified wines), but the same rule applies. The booze has to become part of the dish, it mustn't taste 'raw'.

And don't use any alcohol that you wouldn't drink. A wine that's vinegary in the glass isn't going to do anything for your lovingly made poulet bonne femme. Nobody really talks about alcohol as a storecupboard ingredient and I don't cook with it every night. But my collection of bottles is just opposite the cooker, right where I can reach it for an emergency chicken supper.

turkish-spiced chicken with hot green relish

This dish seems simple, but I can't tell you how much I love it. I'd heard about a Turkish relish-cum-salsa made with crushed green olives and chillies and the desire to try it became overwhelming one night. I have no idea whether this is anything like the Turkish relish I was told about and I don't care; I just bashed everything together, adding and adjusting. When I'd finished I knew I would make this for the rest of my life. It packs a punch, it includes my beloved coriander and is so hot it makes you reach for a beer. I make it a lot to go with lamb as well as chicken.

The chicken and relish are good with rice, of course, but if you're in the mood for a wrap, well, there's nothing better. Make sure you get plenty of cucumber and lettuce in the wrap too, though, as that relish needs taming.

SERVES 4–6

FOR THE CHICKEN

6 tbsp olive oil
½ tsp ground cinnamon
¾ tsp cayenne pepper
1 tsp ground cumin
2 garlic cloves, grated
salt and pepper
6 skinless boneless chicken
   thighs

FOR THE RELISH

2 garlic cloves, chopped
sea salt flakes
1 green chilli
1 red chilli
15g (½oz) coriander,
   roughly chopped
leaves from 8 sprigs of
   mint, torn
70g (2½oz) pitted green olives,
   roughly chopped
6 tbsp extra virgin olive oil
2 tbsp white balsamic vinegar
good squeeze of lemon juice,
   plus lemon wedges to serve

To marinate the chicken, mix the regular oil, cinnamon, cayenne, cumin, garlic and salt and pepper together to make a marinade. Make little slits all over the underside of the pieces of chicken with the point of a knife. Put the chicken into a dish and pour the marinade over, turning to coat. Cover with cling film and put in the fridge. Leave it there for a couple of hours, or overnight. Bring it to room temperature before cooking.

Make the relish just before you cook the chicken. Put the garlic and salt into a mortar and bash it with a pestle until it is crushed. Halve and deseed both chillies and chop them roughly. Add them to the mortar with the coriander, mint and olives and bash everything together, gradually adding the virgin oil and balsamic until you have a rough paste (it should be chunky, not puréed). Add lemon juice to taste and set aside.

Heat a griddle. Lift the chicken out of the marinade, shaking off the excess, and cook it. Start off on a medium heat, cooking the chicken for about two minutes on each side, then reduce the heat to low and cook for another four minutes. The chicken should be cooked right through and singed, but not burnt.

Serve the chicken with lemon wedges, rice or flatbread, a bowl of Greek yogurt and the relish. Cucumber and green salad are good, too.

chicken with marsala, olives and blood oranges

This came about because I like blood oranges so much. I put them with other ingredients that make me think of Sicily – Marsala and olives – and so it was born. It can be hard to find dry Marsala (some people will tell you it doesn't exist), but persevere. When blood oranges aren't in season, use regular oranges.

SERVES 4–6

1 tbsp olive oil
salt and pepper
1 medium skin-on chicken, jointed into 8
2 small red onions, halved and cut into crescent moon-shaped slices
2 garlic cloves, finely chopped
100ml (3½fl oz) dry Marsala
juice of 1 blood orange, plus 2 blood oranges
8 sprigs of thyme
3 tbsp good-quality green olives
a little caster sugar

Preheat the oven to 190°C/375°F/gas mark 5. Heat the olive oil in a broad, shallow casserole in which the chicken joints can lie in a single layer (I use a cast-iron pan). Season the chicken and brown it over a medium-high heat on both sides, skin side first. Be careful not to turn the chicken over before it comes away easily from the base of the pan, otherwise you will tear the skin. Remove the chicken from the pan and set it aside.

Drain off all but a couple of tbsp of the oil and add the onions. Cook over a medium-low heat until they begin to soften. Add the garlic and cook for another two minutes.

Deglaze the pan with the Marsala, stirring round to scrape up all the flavour that's stuck to the base. Add the blood orange juice. Return the chicken – with any juices that have run out of it – to the pan, skin side up. Season and add six of the sprigs of thyme. Bring the liquid underneath the chicken to the boil, then take the pan off the heat and put it in the oven for 20 minutes.

Meanwhile, cut a slice off the bottom and top of each whole blood orange so they have a flat base on which to sit. Using a very sharp knife, cut the peel and pith from each orange, working around the fruit and cutting the peel away in broad slices from top to bottom. Slice the oranges into wheels and flick out any pips you see.

Add the olives to the chicken and lay over the sliced blood oranges. (The oranges should stay on top, out of the liquid.) Sprinkle the orange slices with sugar and return the pan to the oven. Cook for another 20 minutes. The juices under the chicken should have reduced, the orange slices have turned golden, even caramelized in patches, and the chicken be cooked through.

Add the leaves of the remaining two sprigs of thyme – it just lifts the flavour – carefully spooning some of the juices over them. Serve immediately.

chicken with anchovies, lemon and rosemary

Even if you don't like anchovies you will love this dish. The anchovies don't add a 'fishy' taste at all, instead they deepen the flavours of the cooking juices and make the whole dish more complex. Even my kids – who 'hate' anchovies – love this.

SERVES 4

8 large skin-on bone-in chicken thighs, or a mixture of joints
8 banana shallots, peeled
1 tbsp olive oil
4 garlic cloves, finely chopped
really good pinch of chilli flakes
5 anchovies, drained of oil and roughly chopped
3 sprigs of rosemary
75ml (2½fl oz) dry white wine or dry vermouth
finely grated zest and juice of ½ unwaxed lemon

Trim the chicken thighs of scraggy bits of fat to make them neat. Quarter the shallots lengthways. Preheat the oven to 180°C/350°F/gas mark 4.

Heat the oil in a broad shallow pan which can go on the hob and in the oven (and hold the thighs in a single layer without too much room around them). Quickly brown the chicken on both sides over a medium-high heat. You don't want to cook it through, just get some colour on it. Remove the thighs and put them on a plate.

Pour off all but 1 tbsp of the fat from the pan. Add the shallots to the pan and cook for about three minutes to get some colour on these as well, then add three-quarters of the garlic, the chilli and the anchovies. Reduce the heat right down and cook for another four minutes or so, pressing the anchovies with the back of a wooden spoon to help them 'melt' (they just disintegrate).

Add the rosemary, wine and lemon juice and bring to the boil. Take off the heat. Lay the chicken thighs on top of the shallots (the chicken should be skin side up), pour any juices that have come out of the chicken into the pan as well and put into the oven for 35–40 minutes, uncovered.

Check that the chicken is cooked through: when you pierce one of the pieces near the bone the juices that run out should be clear, with no trace of pink. Taste for seasoning. The chilli and anchovies should provide enough, but just make sure. Chop the lemon zest and reserved garlic together very finely and sprinkle over the top. Serve immediately.

roast jerusalem artichokes and chicken with anchovy, walnut and parsley relish

More messing around with anchovies. Here they are not disguised – you know you're eating them – but I am totally hooked on salty-sweet-savoury combinations. Cooks tend to think anchovies are good with lamb, but they work really well with chicken, too.

SERVES 4

FOR THE CHICKEN

900g (2lb) Jerusalem artichokes
5 tbsp extra virgin olive oil
8 skin-on bone-in chicken thighs, or a mixture of joints
salt and pepper
juice of 1 lemon

FOR THE RELISH

1 fat garlic clove, chopped
¼ tsp sea salt flakes
150g (5½oz) walnut pieces
5 anchovies, drained of oil and chopped
75ml (2½fl oz) extra virgin olive oil
1 tsp white balsamic vinegar
4 tbsp finely chopped flat-leaf parsley leaves

Preheat the oven to 200°C/400°F/gas mark 6. Scrub the Jerusalem artichokes well. You don't need to peel them (the skin looks good and has a nice nutty flavour). Cut them in half lengthways and put them in a steamer. Cook for about 10 minutes, then pat them dry.

Heat half the oil in a roasting tin on the hob. Tumble in the Jerusalem artichokes and shake them around to coat in the oil. Brush the rest of the oil on the chicken joints and put these into the tin too, making space for them among the artichokes. Season well and squeeze on the lemon. Roast for 35–40 minutes, shaking the pan every so often. The vegetables should be tender and caramelized in patches and the chicken golden and cooked through.

Meanwhile, make the relish. Put the garlic and salt flakes into a mortar and grind to a paste. Add the walnuts and anchovies and pound until you have a mixture that is partly puréed, partly chunky. Stir in the oil, balsamic, some pepper and the parsley. Either serve the relish on the side (that way people get to choose how much they have), or spoon it over the chicken and artichokes.

chicken rye schnitzel with mustard sauce

Ah, one of the best midweek meals (and – hurrah – one that the kids have taken to as well). If you don't want to make the mustard sauce, just serve some mustard (I prefer English here) on the side. I like it with a sweet-and-sour cucumber salad (see page 87) tossed with dill, or pickled or braised red cabbage. Little waxy potatoes too, please.

SERVES 4

FOR THE SCHNITZEL
8 skinless boneless chicken
    thighs
plain flour
salt and pepper
3 eggs, lightly beaten
200g (7oz) rye breadcrumbs
    (ideally from a loaf which is
    half rye, half wheat)
2 tbsp groundnut oil
½ lemon

FOR THE MUSTARD SAUCE
15g (½oz) unsalted butter
4 shallots, finely chopped
3½ tbsp white wine vinegar
150ml (5fl oz) dry white wine
200ml (7fl oz) double cream
2 tbsp Dijon mustard
good squeeze of lemon juice

Put the thighs between two sheets of greaseproof paper and flatten them with a rolling pin. (Bash them, but not so violently that the chicken flesh starts to break up.)

Set out three broad shallow soup plates (or something similar). Fill one with the flour and season it well, the next with the eggs and the last with the breadcrumbs.

Make the mustard sauce. Melt the butter and gently sauté the shallots until soft. Add the vinegar, whack up the heat and reduce to about 1 tbsp. Add the wine and boil to reduce by half, then add the cream, mustard, lemon and salt and pepper and heat through. If it becomes too thick (the lemon juice will thicken the cream), just let it down with a little water. Set aside to reheat later.

Season the thighs, then dip each one in the flour to coat, then the egg, then press into the rye crumbs. Set them on a non-stick baking sheet as they are ready.

Heat half the groundnut oil in a large non-stick frying pan. Cook the thighs over a medium heat for four minutes on each side. The coating should be golden and the chicken cooked through. Sprinkle with salt and pepper and quickly squeeze lemon juice all over the schnitzel. Quickly reheat the sauce. Serve the chicken immediately with the sauce.

chicken with shaoxing wine, crisp radishes and pickled ginger

A dish that highlights the importance of texture. The sweet chicken is very good against the clean crunch of the radishes and daikon but – to really appreciate it – you should soak the cut radishes in iced water, as that really firms them up. Use Amontillado sherry if you don't have Shaoxing wine and feel free to add sliced chillies at the same time as the ginger and garlic, if you want some heat as well.

SERVES 4

FOR THE CHICKEN

8 skinless boneless chicken
    thighs
115g (4oz) daikon
130g (4¾oz) radishes
2 tbsp groundnut oil
3cm (1¼in) root ginger, peeled
    and shredded
6 garlic cloves, very finely
    sliced
50ml (2fl oz) Shaoxing wine
2½ tbsp dark soy sauce
2 tbsp honey
juice of 1 lime
2 spring onions, finely
    chopped
50g (1¾oz) pickled ginger
    (pink or beige, though pink
    looks better)
2 tsp black or white sesame
    seeds
about 2 tbsp micro leaves, if
    available (purple amaranth,
    cress or pea shoots)

FOR THE MARINADE

3 tbsp dark soy sauce
3 tbsp Shaoxing wine
2 garlic cloves, crushed
pepper

Cut the chicken thighs into chunks (about 2.5cm/1in square) and put into a bowl with the marinade ingredients. Mix everything together, cover with cling film and put in the fridge to marinate for two hours if you have time, 30 minutes if you're pushed. Bring to room temperature before cooking.

Peel the daikon and cut it into thin batons. Trim the radishes and slice them lengthways. Drop these into a bowl of ice cubes and water and leave to crisp up.

Heat 1 tbsp of the oil in a wok or sauté pan until it's really hot, then brown the chicken in three batches, removing the browned chicken as it's ready and putting it into a bowl. It's really important to get a good colour on the chicken.

Add the rest of the oil to the pan, heat it, then add the ginger and garlic and stir-fry until the garlic is pale gold. Deglaze the wok or pan with the Shaoxing wine, then return the browned chicken. Season generously with pepper. Cook for another four minutes, stirring from time to time, then add the soy sauce, honey and 75ml (2½fl oz) of water and cook for another four minutes, tossing the contents of the pan around, until you have enough liquid to just coat the chicken and the chicken is cooked through. Add the lime juice and taste for seasoning.

Put the chicken into a warmed broad, shallow serving bowl. Drain the daikon and radish and quickly pat dry in a clean tea towel. Throw these over the chicken with the spring onions, picked ginger and sesame seeds. Serve immediately, sprinkled with the micro leaves (if using).

chicken, soft spring onions and baby potatoes

As an Irish girl I love spring onions (we call them scallions), as our beloved 'champ' contains nothing more than mashed potatoes, butter and chopped scallions cooked in milk. A sandwich of white bread, butter and chopped spring onions was a favourite childhood snack. But I had never cooked any other dish in which they were dominant. Until this. It's spring-like, with a lovely muted oniony flavour. You can add peas (fresh or frozen, just stir them in towards the end of cooking) and shredded soft lettuce is good, too, just wilting a little in the heat. It's a light, simple sauté, but doesn't seem at all old-fashioned.

SERVES 6–8

8 large skin-on bone-in chicken thighs, or a mixture of joints
400g (14oz) baby waxy potatoes (no need to peel)
10g (¼oz) unsalted butter
½ tbsp olive oil
salt and pepper
450g (1lb) spring onions, roughly chopped
200ml (7fl oz) dry vermouth
3–4 tbsp chicken stock or water
5 tbsp crème fraîche or double cream
1 tbsp chopped chervil leaves (or parsley leaves, though aniseedy chervil is perfect here)

Trim the skin from the chicken thighs so that there are no ragged bits. If the potatoes are any bigger than a walnut, cut them in half.

In a shallow broad pan (such as a sauté pan, something that will hold all the chicken pieces in a single layer) heat the butter and olive oil, season the chicken and brown it over a medium heat until coloured on all sides. You are not trying to cook the chicken through, just colour it. Lift the chicken joints out and put them in a bowl. Pour off all but 3 tbsp of the fat from the pan.

Add 400g (14oz) of the spring onions and cook over a medium heat until they are glossy. Add the vermouth and stock or water and bring to the boil, scraping up all the bits that have stuck to the pan. Put the potatoes into the pan and reduce the heat to medium. Return the chicken, with its juices, cover and cook at a gentle simmer for 20 minutes. Remove the lid and cook for another 20 minutes. The liquid will reduce and the chicken cook right through (you can check by piercing the flesh near the bone with a the tip of a sharp knife; there should be no trace of pink). If you have a lot of liquid left, then remove the chicken and boil the juices to reduce them, but you should have just about enough to give everyone some chicken and a spoonful or two of juice.

Stir in the crème fraîche and the rest of the spring onions. Heat through for a couple of minutes, then scatter the chervil on top and serve.

the art of braising and sautéing

'Casserole' is the sorry name the English-speaking world tends to apply to any dish that is cooked in a bit of liquid. It sounds pretty grim and it's also rather meaningless, because it's so vague. Braises and some sautés involve cooking in liquid – and there are many examples of both within these pages – but they are very different types of dish and there are rules for each of them.

To create a complex interplay of flavours is one of the main aims of cooking and it's at the core of braising, written into the very technique. The French even have a word for it: the verb *mijoter* means 'to cook something slowly on the stove top with the lid on'. In braising you cook meat in liquid, gently and slowly. Slow is the key word, there should only be the vaguest whisper of movement, the occasional bubble breaking the surface in a covered pan. This approach is more often used for tougher cuts of meat as it breaks down connective tissue and chicken doesn't need this, of course, as it's already tender. But the method can still be used for chicken, as something else happens during braising: the meat exudes its flavours into the cooking liquor, while the cooking liquor and the other flavourings in the dish – fat, alcohol, vegetables, herbs – work their way into the heart of the meat. The ingredients slowly imbue each other. Braising produces maximum flavour… and layer upon layer of it.

Most braises (though not all) undergo browning before the liquid is added. The caramelization and 'toasting' that frying in fat produces is vital to the final flavour. But meat won't brown if it's wet, so it's essential to dry it (pat it with kitchen paper, especially if it has been marinating) before it hits the pan. It's important as well not to crowd the pan when you're browning meat, because the moisture created by overcrowding means the chicken will steam instead of brown, so you should do the browning in batches. Avoid using too much fat at this stage or you'll end up with a greasy dish (though some of the fat is usually removed after the browning). Once the meat is browned, onion (and often garlic, too) is cooked in the fat before the chicken is returned to the pan with aromatics and other vegetables. The liquid – stock, water or alcohol, or a mixture of all three – is then added to the chicken and you should choose a snug pot where the meat and liquid are in close contact so the flavours can stay intense. It's best to cook a braise in a pot that doesn't have too large a base area, otherwise the cooking liquor will evaporate too quickly. The cooking juices do reduce as the dish cooks but, if there's too much liquid at the end, you can remove the meat and reduce it by boiling, then return the chicken to warm it through. In the past, braises were thickened with flour; this was either added at the beginning, tossed in round the meat before the liquid was added, or at the end, mashed with butter to form a 'beurre manié' and whisked in. But flour thickening has now gone out of fashion and cooks prefer to reduce the cooking liquor by boiling it.

You probably make chicken sautés all the time without even using a recipe. A chicken sauté is faster to make than a braise and uses significantly less liquid. As with braising, it all starts with browning in fat and the same rules apply: make sure the meat is dry and don't crowd the pan. A proper sauté pan – or a shallow casserole or deep frying pan – is essential. With a sauté, the meat has to be in touch with the base of the pan at all times. After browning, a small amount of liquid can be added and the pan is either covered, or half-covered, during the remaining cooking time. You need to pay attention while a chicken sauté is cooking to make sure it doesn't become dry, adding extra splashes of water or stock when you need them. The aim is to end up with a lovely intense sauce that bathes the chicken and the other elements in the dish.

In a chicken sauté, the other ingredients – mushrooms, seafood, apples, whatever you're using – are added either at the end of cooking time, or part of the way through (they can be cooked with the chicken from the start or in a different pan first). These elements should retain their own distinctive flavour, as should the chicken, so there is none of the slow blending and mellowing you get in a braise (some of the steps are the same, but the fundamental thinking behind a sauté is quite different). As with braising, the chicken can be removed at the end of the cooking time and the cooking liquid reduced by boiling until you get the thickness and consistency that you want. The cooking juices can also be thickened by the addition of cream, or even with a 'liaison' of cream and egg yolks... (though the latter is less common than it once was as it's now considered rather rich).

All this might seem like a lot of instruction to cook very simple dishes, but nothing about either braising or sautéing is difficult. I've written it down because I, for one, was much better at both once I understood why I had to take certain steps. If I had to pick out the absolutely crucial bits of advice, they would be: make sure your chicken is dry so you can brown it properly; and cook both braises and sautés gently (never boil them). So, go forth and make some of the most soothing and feel-good dishes known to man. Chicken forestière with wild mushrooms, carrots and cream (see overleaf) is an earthy and delicious place to start...

chicken forestière

One of those dishes that turns out better than you anticipate. A few dried wild mushrooms, a bag of carrots, some chicken thighs and a dash of cream. Simple ingredients that aren't that expensive. But you end up with a bosky, luxurious panful.

SERVES 4–6

20g (¾oz) dried wild
    mushrooms
salt and pepper
8 skin-on bone-in chicken
    thighs
1 tbsp olive oil
2 small onions, halved and
    cut into thin crescent
    moon-shaped slices
75ml (2½fl oz) Madeira or,
    failing that, dry sherry
215g (7½oz) carrots, peeled
    and cut into batons
200ml (7fl oz) chicken stock
150ml (5fl oz) double cream
150g (5½oz) button or chestnut
    mushrooms, quartered
1 tbsp finely chopped flat-leaf
    parsley leaves

Put the dried mushrooms in a bowl and pour over 50ml (2fl oz) of boiling water. Leave to soak for about 20 minutes while you get on with the chicken.

Season the thighs and heat the oil in a sauté pan. Cook the chicken on both sides to get a good brown colour. Don't turn the pieces over until they can easily be moved, otherwise the skin will tear. You don't need to cook the chicken through, you're just getting a good colour. Remove the chicken from the pan and put in a dish. Pour off all but 1 tbsp of fat from the pan into a bowl (reserve this fat), but don't wash the pan out.

Heat the fat that remains in the pan and sauté the onions until soft and pale gold. Deglaze the pan with the alcohol, scraping with a wooden spoon to dislodge all the flavour from the base.

Add the carrots and the stock, plus the wild mushrooms and their soaking liquor. Bring to the boil, then reduce the heat to a simmer, cover and cook for 10 minutes.

Return the chicken to the pan (together with any juices that have run out of it), placing it skin side up. Cover and cook gently for 20 minutes.

Remove the lid, stir in the cream, return to a simmer again and cook for another 10 minutes with the lid off.

In a separate pan, heat 1 tbsp of the reserved chicken fat and quickly sauté the mushrooms until they are golden brown. The mixture should be dry, so cook until the liquid in the mushrooms has evaporated. Season and toss in with the chicken, stirring gently to combine everything. The 'sauce' should be thick enough to coat the back of a wooden spoon.

Taste for seasoning, though you shouldn't need to adjust it (the reduced chicken stock is quite salty). Scatter on the parsley and serve from the pan in which it was cooked.

poulet bonne femme

There are many versions of this, some using a whole chicken, others using pieces. Some have only bacon and shallots, others include mushrooms as well. The key thing is that it's light and uses white wine. I much prefer it to coq au vin made with red wine. I've always loved the name – 'housewife's chicken' – and I've been cooking it since I was a teenager, when I came across a version in my mum's old Cordon Bleu *part work. It seemed to be the kind of French dish that, with just a little care, I could pull off.*

SERVES 4–6

1 tbsp olive oil

125g (4½oz) bacon lardons (quite chunky bits)

35g (1¼oz) unsalted butter

1 chicken, skin-on, jointed into 8

16 shallots, peeled

275g (9¾oz) really small waxy potatoes (ideally peeled, but don't worry if you're in a hurry)

3 garlic cloves, crushed

200ml (7fl oz) white wine

150ml (5fl oz) chicken stock

1 bouquet garni

salt and pepper

125g (4½oz) small button mushrooms

1 tbsp finely chopped flat-leaf parsley leaves

Heat half the oil in a casserole and sauté the bacon over a medium heat until it is golden all over. Remove with a slotted spoon and set aside. Add half the butter to the pan and brown the chicken on both sides. Don't let the fat burn as you are doing this. Remove the chicken to a plate. Pour off almost all the fat from the casserole, leaving about 1 tbsp behind.

Put the shallots into a saucepan of boiling water, reduce the heat and simmer for four minutes. Drain and pat dry, then put them into the casserole with the potatoes and sauté these in the fat until pale gold. Add the garlic and continue to sauté for two minutes. Pour the wine into the pan and bring to the boil, then immediately reduce the heat and return the chicken and bacon, together with any of the juices that have run out of them. Pour in the stock, add the bouquet garni and season. Bring it all to the boil, then reduce the heat to a gentle simmer. Cook for 40 minutes, or until the chicken is tender and cooked through (when you pierce the flesh nearest the bone with the tip of a sharp knife the juices that run from the chicken should be clear, with no trace of pink). The potatoes should be completely tender, too.

Meanwhile, melt the rest of the butter and oil in a frying pan and sauté the mushrooms briskly so they get a really good colour. Allow their juices to evaporate. Season. Add them to the chicken about 15 minutes before the end of the cooking time.

Check for seasoning, scatter on the parsley and serve immediately.

chicken with riesling, leeks and grapes

The richest of the French chicken dishes in this chapter and a good Friday night treat for supper with friends. If you're not partial to grapes you can use the same recipe, sauté about 125g (4½oz) of quartered button mushrooms once the dish is cooked and gently stir them in instead.

SERVES 4

1 tbsp olive oil

15g (½oz) unsalted butter

salt and pepper

4 skin-on bone-in chicken legs (drumsticks and thighs attached)

1 onion, very finely chopped

375ml (13fl oz) dry Riesling

3 medium-large leeks

150ml (5fl oz) chicken stock

3 sprigs of thyme, plus leaves from 2 sprigs of thyme

1 bay leaf

150ml (5fl oz) double cream

60g (3oz) seedless green grapes, not too big

squeeze of lemon juice

Heat the oil and butter in a large sauté pan over a medium heat, season the chicken pieces and brown them on both sides until they are a good golden colour. Don't turn the chicken until it is easy to move, or the skin will tear. It will take about eight minutes to brown both sides properly.

Remove the chicken and pour off all but 1 tbsp of the fat in the pan. Add the onion and cook over a medium-low heat until it is soft but not coloured. Add the Riesling and bring to the boil, stirring to dislodge the essences stuck to the bottom of the pan and reducing the wine by half.

Remove the dark leaves from the tops of the leeks and any coarse outer leaves. Trim the bases. Cut each leek into neat lengths of about 4cm (1½in). Wash these, keeping them intact.

Add the stock to the pan and return to the boil. Reduce the heat to a very gentle simmer, add the herbs and leeks and return the chicken with any juices that have run out of it. Cover the pan and cook for 15 minutes. Remove the leeks carefully with a slotted spoon – they should be tender by now – and set aside. Continue to cook the chicken for another 20–25 minutes, then remove the chicken and reduce the cooking liquid by boiling; you want to end up with about 150ml (5fl oz).

Add the cream and the grapes and bring to the boil to cook the grapes and reduce the sauce. You should end up with a sauce that just coats the back of a wooden spoon. Remove the herbs. Add the lemon juice and taste for seasoning. Return the chicken and leeks to the cream sauce and gently heat through. Serve with the extra thyme leaves sprinkled over the top.

the spice route *scented, perfumed, hot*

roopa's lemon grass and turmeric chicken with potato salad and date and tamarind chutney

One of my favourite dishes in the book, this recipe comes from my friend Roopa Gulati. Her mum used to make it. It is actually very simple to cook – it's just spiced roast chicken with dressed potatoes, after all – but it is satisfying on every level: it looks like a painting when you set it on the table (all those dark colours); has contrasting flavours (slightly bitter turmeric beside sweet dates); and is an Indian dish that has a fairly limited ingredients list so it's not time-consuming to make. You ideally need fresh turmeric; it looks like a skinny, bright-coloured root ginger. You'll find it in larger supermarkets and ethnic shops. If you can't find it, use 1 tbsp of ground turmeric instead, though it doesn't make a paste. I couldn't publish this recipe without its delicious accompaniments, so you'll find them on the next page.

SERVES 6

4cm (1½in) fresh turmeric
2 lemon grass stalks
3 red chillies, chopped
60g (3oz) galangal or root ginger, peeled and chopped
1 tsp salt
4 tbsp rice vinegar
2 tbsp vegetable oil
1½ tsp cracked black peppercorns
1.5kg (3lb 5oz) chicken
2 limes, halved
small bunch of Thai basil (or mint if you can't find Thai basil)
125ml (4fl oz) chicken stock (optional)

The day before, peel the turmeric and roughly chop (best to wear clean kitchen gloves; that yellow colour stains everything). Remove the coarse outer layers from the lemon grass and trim the top and base. Chop the rest – the softer bit of the lemon grass – as finely as you can. Combine the turmeric and lemon grass with the chillies, the galangal and salt. Blitz in a food processor or blender with the vinegar and oil and add the cracked pepper.

Make slashes in the chicken on its breasts and legs with a small sharp knife. With gloved hands, rub the paste all over the chicken, pushing it into the slashes and inside the bird, too. Cover loosely with cling film and marinate the chicken overnight in the fridge. Bring it to room temperature before cooking. Truss the bird, if you like; it does make it look neat.

The next day, preheat the oven to 180°C/350°F/gas mark 4. Stuff the cavity with three lime halves and the Thai basil, squeezing the remaining lime half over the bird. Roast in the oven for 1 hour 15 minutes. Three-quarters of the way through the cooking time, add the stock or the same amount of water to the tin and scrape the sediment off the bottom to mix in with the liquid.

Serve the chicken with the juices from the pan, the potato salad overleaf and a cucumber raita.

cumin and lime-scented potato salad with date and tamarind chutney

It might seem odd to drizzle a 'chutney' over a salad, but this is a smooth Indian chutney, rather than the thick, chunky Anglo-Indian variety.

The chutney recipe makes about 300ml (½ pint), which is more than you need for the potato salad, but it's difficult to work with smaller quantities. The extra can be frozen in batches.

The potatoes and chutney are actually lovely on their own with some cucumber raita, but both also make brilliant side dishes for any chicken roasted with Indian spices and they're especially wonderful with the chicken on the previous page.

SERVES 6 AS A SIDE DISH

FOR THE CHUTNEY

150g (5½oz) tamarind paste

150g (5½oz) pitted dates, chopped

150g (5½oz) jaggery or soft dark brown sugar

1 tsp ground ginger

½ tsp garam masala

1½ tsp cumin seeds, toasted and ground

FOR THE POTATO SALAD

500g (1lb 2oz) small waxy potatoes

juice of 1 lime

1 red onion, finely chopped

½ tsp cracked black peppercorns

1 green chilli, deseeded and finely chopped

1 red chilli, deseeded and finely chopped

2½ tsp cumin seeds, toasted and ground (see page 66)

2 tbsp chopped coriander leaves

leaves from 6 sprigs of mint, torn

Start with the chutney. Put the tamarind, dates, jaggery or sugar and 500ml (18fl oz) of water into a pan and bring to the boil. Reduce the heat and simmer until the dates are really soft and the mixture has reduced by about half.

Remove the pan from the heat and leave to cool. Stir in the spices and whizz in a food processor until smooth. Add a dash of water if it's too thick; you want something with a coating consistency.

Boil the potatoes until tender. Halve each one and tip into a serving bowl. Add the lime juice, red onion, cracked pepper, chillies and cumin and leave to cool (you can serve this warm or at room temperature). Toss in the herbs and drizzle with about 50ml (2fl oz) of the chutney. Serve.

jamaican chicken curry with sweet love apples and rum

Spicy and coconutty, Jamaican curry really can contain whatever vegetables you have to hand, so you can use sweet potato instead of pumpkin, or add peppers or carrots. It can also be hotter, so up the chilli content if you want to. My own additions to the traditional Jamaican version are caramelized tomatoes (tomatoes are known as 'love apples' there) – I like the sweetness they bring at the end – and a good slosh of rum (just enough to be detectable). I mean, why not?

SERVES 6

650g (1lb 7oz) skinless boneless chicken thighs or leg meat, cut into big chunks

2 tbsp curry powder

75ml (2½fl oz) lime juice, plus the juice of ½ lime, plus the finely grated zest of 2

3 tbsp coconut oil (or any other oil you prefer)

salt and pepper

500g (1lb 2oz) butternut squash, peeled, deseeded and cut into chunks

250g (9oz) potato, peeled and cut into chunks

2 tsp ground allspice

3 garlic cloves, roughly chopped

2cm (¾in) root ginger, peeled and grated

2 red chillies, halved, deseeded and shredded

6 spring onions, chopped

4 sprigs of thyme, plus the leaves of 1 sprig

400ml can of coconut milk

4 large tomatoes, chopped

1 tsp soft light brown sugar

3 tbsp rum

Put the chicken, 1 tbsp of the curry powder and the 75ml (2½fl oz) of lime juice into a bowl. Toss together with your hands then cover with cling film, put in the fridge and leave to marinate overnight (or for at least four hours). Bring it to room temperature before cooking.

Heat 2 tbsp of the oil in a heavy-based casserole, season the chicken with salt and pepper and, working in batches, brown the chicken all over. Remove with a slotted spoon and set aside. Add the squash and potato and cook over a medium heat to get a little colour on them for about six minutes. Now add the rest of the curry powder, the allspice, garlic, ginger, chillies and spring onions and cook for about two minutes, stirring.

Return the chicken, together with any juices which have run out of it, to the pan with the marinade. Add the 4 sprigs of thyme, the lime zest and coconut milk and season. Heat until the mixture is at a gentle simmer, then leave it to cook for about 30 minutes. The chicken and vegetables will become tender and the liquid will reduce.

About five minutes before the curry is ready, heat the rest of the oil in a frying pan and add the tomatoes. Season. Cook them until they are soft and a lot of their liquid has evaporated. Add the sugar and allow the tomatoes to caramelize a little. Add these to the curry. If the sauce seems a little thin, then gently mash some of the squash and potatoes with a fork to thicken the sauce. Add the rum and heat through. Check for seasoning. Although you will feel like reaching for the coriander, it's not right for this: thyme is the thing. Add a final sprinkling of it and a really generous squeeze of lime juice.

pollo cubano with fried eggs and plantains

An oddity to us, perhaps – chicken, eggs and something that tastes like bananas – but this is such a satisfying dish (though, admittedly, I do not always choose to have the egg). It's a doddle to make with leftover chicken (just heat it in a frying pan, then add it to the rice) but so good with juicy fried thighs, as here. Embellish freely. Try the Smashed avocado (see page 16), the Avocado salsa (see page 82) and – a must for me – Chilli sauce (see overleaf).

Oh, before you complain that there are rather a lot of pans involved: sometimes it's worth it.

SERVES 6

200g (7oz) long-grain rice
3 tbsp groundnut or sunflower
    oil, plus more to fry the eggs
    and plantains
250g (9oz) tomatoes, chopped
2 garlic cloves, finely chopped
4 spring onions, chopped
2 red chillies, halved and finely
    sliced (I don't deseed them)
¼ tsp dried oregano
1 tsp ground cumin
salt and pepper
4 skinless boneless chicken
    thighs
2 ripe plantains
juice of 3 limes
6 small eggs
3 tbsp chopped coriander
    leaves

Put the rice into a saucepan and add water to come just 2.5cm (1in) above the level of the rice. Bring to the boil, then boil vigorously until the surface looks 'pitted', as if the rice has lots of little holes in it. Reduce the heat to very low, cover and cook for about 15 minutes. Make sure the rice doesn't scorch on the base of the pan.

Meanwhile, heat 1 tbsp of the oil in a large frying pan and cook the tomatoes for about five minutes. Add the garlic, spring onions, chillies, oregano and cumin and cook for another two minutes. Cover and leave in the pan.

Heat 2 tbsp of the oil in another frying pan. Season the chicken thighs and cook them over a medium-high heat to get a good colour on both sides, then reduce the heat and continue until they are cooked through. It will take about eight minutes in all. Cut into strips and keep in the pan (covered) so they stay warm.

Heat enough oil in a frying pan to come to 2cm (¾in) deep. Peel the skins from the plantains and slice into rounds about 1cm (½in) thick. When a drop of water sizzles in the oil, add the plantain slices and cook until the undersides are golden brown. Turn and cook on the other side until golden and slightly caramelized at the edges. It takes about five minutes in all. Lift out with a slotted spoon and put on to kitchen paper to soak up excess oil. Pat the top of the slices too. Sprinkle with salt and pepper and squeeze on the juice of one of the limes. They can sit happily while you fry the eggs.

Add the drained rice and chicken to the pan with the tomatoes. Heat through well while you fry the eggs. Stir the coriander into the rice mixture and squeeze on the remaining lime juice.

Serve the chicken and rice with the plantains and eggs.

hainan chicken rice

Healthy, 'clean' and with a hot sauce that will knock your socks off, this is a great lunch for a crowd. I love that it's plain, but lifted by strong flavours: chilli, ginger and spring onion. It is of Chinese origin and most often found in Malaysia and Singapore, though it's popular in Vietnam and Thailand, too.

SERVES 6

FOR THE CHICKEN

200g (7oz) spring onions
    (about 2 bunches)
5 garlic cloves, sliced
125g (4½oz) root ginger, sliced
1.5kg (3lb 5oz) chicken
75ml (2½fl oz) dark soy sauce
25ml (1fl oz) light soy sauce
1 tbsp toasted sesame oil
1 large cucumber
leaves from 15g (½oz) bunch
    of coriander
about 3 tbsp Crispy fried
    shallots (optional;
    see page 220)

FOR THE CHILLI SAUCE

8 red chillies, deseeded and
    roughly chopped
30g (1oz) root ginger, peeled
    and roughly chopped
4 garlic cloves, chopped
2 tsp caster sugar
2 tbsp groundnut oil
juice of 1 lime
½ tsp fish sauce

FOR THE RICE

15g (½oz) unsalted butter
15g (½oz) root ginger, grated
3 garlic cloves, finely chopped
425g (15oz) Thai jasmine rice,
    well washed and drained
salt

Start with the chicken. Put 4 litres (7 pints) of water, half the spring onions, the garlic and ginger into a large saucepan and bring to the boil. Add the chicken. When it returns to the boil, reduce the heat and simmer for 10 minutes. Cover the pan, place it over the lowest heat and leave to cook for 50 minutes.

Take the chicken out of the stock and remove the breasts. Return the rest of the bird to its stock, increase the heat and simmer gently for another 10 minutes. Reserve 750ml (1¼ pints) of the stock then leave the chicken, covered, in the pot.

To make the chilli sauce, put all the ingredients in a food processor and whizz. Scrape into a serving bowl.

For the rice, melt the butter in a saucepan and sauté the ginger and garlic for about three minutes. Add the rice and sauté for another five minutes, stirring it round in the buttery juices. Add the reserved stock, bring to the boil and cook until the rice looks pitted. Reduce the heat to its lowest, cover and cook for 20 minutes. Remove from the heat, still covered.

Mix the two soy sauces together with the sesame oil. Trim the remaining spring onions and cut into lengths on the diagonal. Put half of these on a small plate. Halve the cucumber lengthways, slice very finely and arrange on another plate.

When you're ready to serve, put the chicken breasts back in with the rest of the chicken, bring to the simmer to heat through, then cut the chicken into pieces (drumsticks, halved thighs and so on; it's a good idea to have a cleaver on hand). Increase the heat under the stock and reduce so it has a stronger flavour. Put all the chicken on a platter with the breasts – cut in several slices – on top. Spoon some of the soy-sesame dressing over, then sprinkle with the other half of the spring onions. Sprinkle with the cucumber and Crispy fried shallots (if using).

Serve the chicken with the rest of the dressing, chilli sauce, rice and vegetables. Serve the broth in bowls, with the coriander.

tajine of chicken, caramelized onions and pears

This is one of the Moroccan tajines in Claudia Roden's lovely book, Arabesque. *I've changed it very little. As it's sweet, I like it served with couscous or rice that has had chopped preserved lemon stirred through it (as well as herbs). It needs something fresh and sharp as a contrast.*

SERVES 4–6

500g (1lb 2oz) shallots or baby onions
2 tbsp olive oil
salt and pepper
1.7kg (3lb 12oz) chicken, skin-on, jointed into 8
1 large onion, roughly chopped
1 tsp ground ginger
1 tsp ground cinnamon
good pinch of saffron strands
1½ tbsp runny honey
15g (½oz) unsalted butter
4 small sweet ripe pears, peeled, quartered and cored
flaked almonds or sesame seeds, toasted, to serve

To peel the shallots or baby onions, blanch them in boiling water for five minutes, then drain. When they're cool enough to handle, peel off the skins and trim the root ends.

Heat the olive oil in a pan large enough to hold all the chicken pieces in one layer. Season the chicken and brown it all over. You aren't trying to cook it through, just get some good colour. Remove to a plate.

Drain off all but about 1 tbsp of fat from the pan and add the onion. Cook over a medium heat until soft and golden. Add the ginger and cinnamon and cook for two minutes. Pour on about 250ml (9fl oz) of boiling water and add the saffron, stirring to help dissolve the strands. Return the chicken to the pan and cook, covered, over a low heat, for about 15 minutes. Add the shallots or baby onions and continue to cook, covered, for another 20–25 minutes. (The chicken is cooked when it is tender and, when a thick piece is pierced near the bone with the tip of a sharp knife, the juices that run have no trace of pink.) Turn the chicken pieces and stir gently every so often. Add a little more water if you need to.

Lift out the chicken and set aside. Stir the honey into the pan. Cook, uncovered, until the liquid has really evaporated and the onions are brown and caramelized and so soft that you could crush them, as the Moroccans say, 'with your tongue'. At the same time, melt the butter in a frying pan and sauté the pears over a medium heat until they are tender and golden. Season.

Return the chicken to the pan for a final time, spoon the onions on top and heat through. Put the pears on top, sprinkle with the almonds or sesame seeds and serve.

guisado de pollo

This is based on a Dominican dish, though I've made my own additions (the traditional version doesn't use chipotles) and left out the green olives that often appear. If you don't want to buy a pineapple, it's okay here to use pineapple canned in natural juice (not in syrup!). It does make things easier. Despite the long list of ingredients, this is a an easy supper dish.

SERVES 6

2 tbsp olive oil

800g (1lb 12oz) skinless boneless chicken thighs

salt and pepper

75g (2¾oz) pumpkin, cut into 2.5cm (1in) chunks

400g (14oz) waxy potatoes, cut into 1cm (½in) chunks

1 onion, roughly chopped

1 red pepper, halved, deseeded and chopped

6 garlic cloves, grated

4 tsp ground cumin

½ medium-sized pineapple, peeled, cored and cut into small chunks

400g can of tomatoes in thick juice

1 tsp soft dark brown sugar

2 canned chipotles in adobo sauce, finely chopped, or 3 tbsp chipotle paste

3 sprigs of thyme

500ml (18fl oz) chicken stock

1 jalapeño chilli, halved lengthways and deseeded

2 tbsp capers, rinsed of vinegar or brine

juice of 1 lime

small bunch of coriander, roughly chopped

Heat half the oil in a casserole and brown the chicken on both sides over a medium-high heat, in batches if necessary so as not to crowd the pan, seasoning as you do so. You are not trying to cook the chicken through, just colour it well. Remove the pieces and put them into a dish.

Put the pumpkin and potatoes into the oil in the pan and cook for about five minutes, until the vegetables are just becoming tinged with gold. Remove with a slotted spoon and set aside. Add the rest of the oil to the casserole and sauté the onion and pepper until they are softening and the onion is pale gold, about eight minutes. Add the garlic and cumin and cook for another two minutes.

Stir in the pineapple, tomatoes, sugar, chipotles, thyme and chicken stock and season. Bring gradually to the boil, then reduce the heat to a simmer. Cut the chicken into strips and add to the pot along with any of the juices that have run out of it, along with the pumpkin and potatoes. Put the jalapeño into the pot too, stirring gently, then leave everything to simmer, uncovered, for about 25 minutes. Stir it a few times during the cooking. The vegetables should be soft and the cooking juices should have thickened.

Add the capers and lime juice and taste for seasoning. Stir in the coriander and serve.

indonesian roast spiced chicken with mango and tomato salad

Here the chicken is golden brown and coconutty, the salad is fresh. If you hate shrimp paste – and some people can't abide it – use fish sauce instead. It isn't authentic but it's better than not making this dish at all (and it's not a bad substitute).

SERVES 4

FOR THE CHICKEN

1.5kg (3lb 5oz) chicken, skin-on, spatchcocked
6 tbsp soy sauce
juice of 2 limes, plus lime wedges to serve
2 onions, roughly chopped
8 garlic cloves, chopped
4 tsp sambal olek
½ tsp dried shrimp paste
½ tsp ground black pepper
400ml can of coconut milk

FOR THE SALAD

1 large green mango
1 tbsp fish sauce
1 tbsp caster sugar
juice of 2 limes
250g (9oz) sweet, firm-but-ripe cherry tomatoes, quartered
35g (1¼oz) fresh coconut, grated
1 red chilli, halved, deseeded and finely sliced
1 green chilli, halved, deseeded and finely sliced
freshly ground black pepper
small bunch of coriander, very roughly chopped

Cut the chicken in half lengthways (removing the parson's nose) and trim any excess skin to make it neat. Put the soy sauce, lime juice, onions, garlic, sambal olek, shrimp paste and pepper into a blender. Blend, adding just enough water to make a thick purée (you'll have to stop every so often, stir and blitz again; the mixture should be as smooth as possible).

Make incisions in the undersides of the chicken (don't cut the skin) and put the pieces into a dish. Spread the purée all over it, on both sides, cover with cling film and marinate in the fridge for about four hours, turning the pieces halfway through.

Preheat the oven to 190°C/375°F/gas mark 5. Put the coconut milk into a large frying or sauté pan set over a medium heat. Add the chicken halves and cook – uncovered and skin side up – for 10 minutes. Don't let the coconut milk boil. Baste with the juices and marinade as the chicken cooks. Turn the chicken over, reduce the heat and do the same thing on the other side.

Transfer the chicken – skin side down – to a rack set in a roasting tin. Pour in enough water to lie 2cm (¾in) deep. Cook in the oven for 20 minutes, then turn the chicken and cook for another 20 minutes, skin side up. It will turn golden brown. Check the chicken is cooked: when you pierce the thickest part near the bone, the juices should run clear with no trace of pink.

When the chicken is nearly finished cooking, make the salad. Peel the mango and cut off the cheeks (the plump bits on each side of the stone). Remove as much of the rest of the flesh as you can neatly, without bruising. Cut into 1cm (½in) cubes. Mix the fish sauce, sugar and lime juice until the sugar has dissolved. Put the mango and tomatoes into a serving dish and add all the other ingredients. Toss everything together.

Serve the chicken with lime wedges, the salad and some rice.

korean fried chicken wings

Before anyone points out that my last book was on healthy eating and I now have Korean fried chicken on the menu, I'm not suggesting you eat this every day. I don't even eat it once a month. But when I do, I bloody love it. Hot, sweet, dark, messy and wickedly good. I am not a fan of deep-frying – I get the children to stand by with a fire blanket when the fat gets to that rolling stage – but sometimes it is worth the effort (and I did try various 'oven-baked' versions to make life easier for you, but they didn't cut the mustard). This is Friday night food, it's not for cooking when you're in a hurry. Best if two of you can share the deep-frying duties. Get the beers in, guys…

SERVES 4

FOR THE SAUCE

4 garlic cloves, grated
2.5cm (1in) root ginger, peeled
    and grated
4½ tbsp Korean chilli paste
    (gochujang)
2 tbsp dark soy sauce
1 tbsp rice vinegar
3 tbsp soft dark brown sugar
1 tbsp fish sauce
1 tbsp sesame oil

FOR THE CHICKEN

75g (2¾oz) plain flour
4 tbsp rice flour
1.5kg (3lb 5oz) chicken wings,
    tips removed if you prefer
vegetable oil, to deep-fry
sesame seeds, to sprinkle
2 spring onions, finely
    chopped

Put everything for the sauce into a saucepan and heat gently, stirring a little to help the sugar dissolve. Bring to the boil, then reduce the heat and simmer for five minutes. It should be quite thick.

Cook the chicken in three batches so as not to overcrowd the pan (if you do, the temperature of the oil drops immediately).

Mix the plain flour and rice flour together in a bowl. Toss the chicken wings in this and shake off the excess. Put about 7.5cm (3in) of oil into a deep pan and heat to 160°C (325°F). Add one batch of chicken wings and cook for six minutes at this temperature (keep an eye on the temperature, reducing the heat or pulling the pan off the heat for a little while if necessary). As each batch is done, remove to a metal rack set over layers of kitchen paper.

Now heat the oil to 180°C (350°F), put the wings back (again in three batches) and cook them for another five minutes. Remove again to the rack and let the excess oil drip off on to the kitchen paper. Paint them all over with the sauce, put them on a plate and sprinkle on the sesame seeds and spring onions. Serve the rest of the sauce on the side.

west african chicken and peanut stew

This is quick to make, rich and warming. And children seem to love it. Peanut stews are found all over West Africa. They used to be made with native groundnuts before the peanut arrived there in the 16th century. You can make your own peanut butter for this — that's what they do there — but since this is, for me, an easy midweek meal I reach for a jar.

The texture of African peanut stews varies depending on the region — some are thin, others thick — and they are served with millet or rice. Vegetables vary; okra (which I hate) often appears, so use it if you like it. You can also use carrots or sweet potatoes. The important thing is to cut the richness of the peanuts with spices — especially chilli — and lime juice. Coriander is my own addition as, in Africa, it is often served with khouthia *(hibiscus leaf conserve), which is hard to find.*

SERVES 6–8

300g (10½oz) crunchy peanut butter
500ml (18fl oz) chicken stock
3 tbsp flavourless vegetable oil
800g (1lb 12oz) skinless boneless chicken thighs
2 large onions, thinly sliced
6 garlic cloves, finely chopped
30g (1oz) root ginger, grated
3 tsp ground coriander
3 tsp ground cumin
1 tsp turmeric
½ tsp ground cinnamon
½ tsp ground allspice
1 Scotch bonnet chilli, stalk removed, chopped
400g can of chopped tomatoes
2 bay leaves
salt and plenty of pepper
325g (11½oz) pumpkin, deseeded and peeled
2 red peppers, sliced
juice of ½–1 lime
about 3 tbsp chopped coriander leaves
1 red chilli, deseeded and very finely sliced (optional)

To make the peanut sauce, put the peanut butter in a jug. Heat the chicken stock to boiling, pour it over and stir it to melt the peanut butter. Keep stirring until it has dissolved. Set this aside.

Heat the oil in a casserole and brown the chicken on each side over a medium heat. Do this in batches or you won't get a good colour; you are not trying to cook the chicken, just colour it well. As the chicken is browned, lift it out and put it into a dish.

Add the onions and fry until golden, about 10 minutes. Add the garlic and ginger and cook for two minutes, then add all the dry spices and cook for another two minutes. Stir in the Scotch bonnet, canned tomatoes and bay leaves. Season.

Cut the pumpkin flesh into 2cm (¾in) chunks and add to the pot with the peppers and the peanut mixture. Bring to the boil, season and reduce the heat to a simmer. Cook for 10 minutes.

Return the chicken to the pan, with any juices that have come out of it. Cook gently — partially covered — until the chicken is cooked through and the vegetables are tender. It will take about 25 minutes. Stir fairly frequently, or the peanut mixture tends to stick to the pan.

Your mixture should be pretty thick and rich. If it seems a little thin, remove the chicken with a slotted spoon and continue to cook until it reaches the consistency you want, then return the chicken and heat it through. Add the lime juice, taste, then adjust the seasoning if it needs it.

Scatter the top with the coriander and chilli (unless you have found the dish too hot already) and serve with boiled rice.

chicken with rice, sweet potato and pepper stuffing, coriander and coconut sauce

Roast chicken and stuffing – eastern style – with coconut 'gravy'. And no hassle.

SERVES 6

FOR THE CHICKEN

125g (4½oz) basmati rice

1 tbsp groundnut, sunflower
　or rapeseed oil

½ onion, very finely chopped

3 garlic cloves, grated

1 red chilli, halved, deseeded
　and finely chopped

150g (5½oz) sweet potato,
　peeled and cut into cubes

1 small red pepper, cut into
　squares

1 bunch of coriander, stalks
　and leaves separated and
　finely chopped

finely grated zest of 1 lime

salt and pepper

1.8kg (4lb) chicken

10g (¼oz) unsalted butter

FOR THE SAUCE

½ tbsp groundnut, sunflower
　or rapeseed oil

1 small onion, finely chopped

2 x 160ml cans of coconut
　cream

juice of 1 lime, plus more if
　needed

Put the rice into a saucepan and add water to come just 2.5cm (1in) above the level of the rice. Bring to the boil, then boil vigorously until the surface looks 'pitted' as if the rice has lots of little holes in it. Reduce the heat to very low, cover and cook for about 15 minutes. Make sure the rice doesn't scorch on the base of the pan.

Meanwhile, heat the oil in a frying pan and add the onion. Cook for about eight minutes, until the onion is softening and slightly golden. Add the garlic and chilli and cook for another two minutes. Scrape this into a bowl and add the sweet potato and pepper to the frying pan. Cook until the sweet potato is just starting to get tinged at the edges; it doesn't have to be soft, it will cook in the stuffing. Add this to the onion with the drained rice, the coriander stalks, lime zest and seasoning. Leave to cool. Preheat the oven to 180°C/350°F/gas mark 4.

Stuff the chicken with the rice mixture, pushing it down well into the cavity. Tie the legs together if you want to. Put into a roasting tin, smear the butter on top, season and roast in the hot oven for 1 hour 20 minutes.

For the sauce, heat the oil in a frying pan and gently sauté the onion until it is soft but not coloured. Pour off the cooking juices from the chicken into a glass jug and skim the fat from the top. Add the chicken juices and coconut cream to the pan, season and bring to just under the boil. Add the lime juice and coriander leaves. Taste to check if you need either more lime or a bit more seasoning.

Serve the chicken with the stuffing and the coconut sauce. I don't serve any more starch – there is enough in the stuffing – but stir-fried greens are good on the side.

parsee chicken with apricots

Gorgeously sweet and sour and very easy to put together. Traditionally this is served with potato straws, but I like it with brown rice and raita.

SERVES 4

2 whole dried Kashmiri
  chillies
5cm (2in) cinnamon stick,
  slightly broken up
2 tsp cumin seeds
seeds from 4 cardamom pods
8 skinless bone-in chicken
  thighs
3cm (1¼in) root ginger, peeled
  and grated
4 garlic cloves, grated
2 tbsp sunflower or groundnut
  oil
2 large onions, thinly sliced
150g (5½oz) tomatoes,
  chopped
1 tsp ground coriander
½ tsp turmeric
1 tsp garam masala
150g (5½oz) dried apricots,
  very roughly chopped
3 tbsp white wine vinegar
1 tbsp jaggery or soft dark
  brown sugar
salt and pepper
chopped mint or coriander
  leaves, to serve
toasted flaked almonds, to
  serve (optional)

Put the whole spices into a frying pan and toast them over a medium heat for two minutes. Grind, either in a mortar and pestle or a small food processor.

Put the chicken in a bowl and add half the spice blend and half the ginger and garlic. Rub this well into the chicken, cover, refrigerate and marinate for an hour (if you have time you can leave it overnight and cook the next day). Bring it to room temperature before cooking.

Heat the oil in a sauté pan and brown the chicken until it has a good colour on both sides. Remove the chicken and set aside. Cook the onions in the same pan until they are golden brown; this will take some time but you need it for both taste and colour. Stir in the tomatoes and cook for another five minutes, then add the remaining ginger and garlic, the rest of the toasted spice blend and the ground coriander, turmeric and garam masala and cook for two minutes, stirring from time to time.

Return the chicken to the pan together with any juices that have run out of it, pour in 200ml (7fl oz) of water and add the apricots, vinegar and jaggery or sugar. Season with salt and pepper. Bring to the boil, cover, reduce the heat to low and simmer for 30 minutes or until the chicken is cooked through.

If the mixture seems to be getting too dry as it cooks, add a little more water, but don't drown it as the final dish should be thick and jammy. If it seems a bit thin at the end of the cooking time, remove the chicken, boil the liquid to reduce it, then return the chicken and heat it through again. Serve scattered with the herbs and the almonds (if using).

vietnamese caramelized ginger chicken

It's important here to get the sugar to caramelize, otherwise you miss the depth of flavour this dish is supposed to have and will also end up with a bowlful that is rather too sweet.

SERVES 4

6 skin-on bone-in chicken thighs
3 tbsp fish sauce
4 tbsp caster sugar
8 garlic cloves, crushed
50g (1¾oz) root ginger, peeled and grated
2 red chillies, 1 sliced with seeds, the other halved, deseeded and sliced
1 tbsp groundnut or sunflower oil
1 onion, halved and cut into small crescent moon-shaped wedges
400ml (14fl oz) chicken stock
juice of 1–2 limes
2 spring onions, finely sliced on the diagonal
small handful of coriander, roughly chopped

Remove the excess fat and skin from each thigh and cut each in half, through the bone (a meat cleaver is best for this but a heavy knife will also do). Put these in a bowl with the fish sauce, 1 tbsp of the sugar, the garlic, ginger and the sliced whole chilli. Turn everything over to make sure the chicken gets coated. Cover with cling film and put in the fridge to marinate. It ideally needs four hours, though overnight is even better. Bring it to room temperature before cooking.

Heat the oil in a sauté pan and fry the chicken over a medium heat on all sides to get a good colour (reserve the marinade). Remove the chicken with a slotted spoon and set aside. Add the onion to the pan and fry until it is just beginning to get a good colour. Add it to the chicken.

Drain any excess oil from the pan, but don't clean it. Add the rest of the sugar and 2 tbsp of water and heat until the sugar turns to caramel; you must take it far enough so that the sugar caramelizes (otherwise you will just have a sweet sauce), but not so far that it burns. The colour and smell should tell you when you get there. Immediately add the stock and the juice of 1 lime. Bring to the boil, then add the chicken, onion and reserved marinade. Reduce the heat and simmer, uncovered, for 15 minutes, or until the chicken is cooked through and the juices are nice and glossy round the meat.

Stir in the rest of the chilli, the spring onions and the coriander. Check to see whether you need more lime. Serve immediately with rice and stir-fried greens.

chicken in bitter orange and guava adobo

This is the kind of food everyone salivates over as soon as you take it to the table; it is so dark and glossy and smells great. You can get guava jelly in large supermarkets and ethnic shops (or online at www. theasiancookshop.co.uk) but, if you don't want to buy it, use quince (or even apple) jelly. It would be a shame not to cook this because you can't find it. Ideally, use bitter Seville oranges but, when they're not in season, use half orange and half lime juice.

The recipe is adapted from an outstanding American book called Gran Cocina Latina *by Maricel Presilla. She uses the marinade on pork, which is also fantastic.*

SERVES 6

FOR THE MARINADE

35g (1¼oz) dry ancho chillies
35g (1¼oz) dry guajillo chillies
6 large garlic cloves, chopped
1 red chilli, deseeded, chopped
2 tsp ground cumin
1 tsp dried oregano
½ tsp smoked paprika
¼ tsp fennel seeds, crushed
150ml (5fl oz) Seville orange
    juice
1 tbsp sherry vinegar
1½ tbsp guava jelly
1 tbsp muscovado sugar
½ tsp salt and pepper
175ml (6fl oz) dry sherry

FOR THE CHICKEN

1.8kg (4lb) chicken
500g (1lb 2oz) sweet potatoes,
    peeled and cut into chunks
400g (14oz) waxy potatoes,
    peeled and cut into chunks
1 large red onion, in slim wedges
handful of coriander leaves

FOR THE GLAZE

2 tbsp guava jelly
1 tbsp soft dark brown sugar
2 tbsp lime juice

Heat a frying pan and toast the dried chillies in it for about 25 seconds on each side. Put them into a saucepan, cover with boiling water and simmer for 15 minutes. Drain, remove the stalks and put the chillies in a food processor with everything else for the marinade, except using only 75ml (2½fl oz) of the sherry. Whizz to a paste. Put the chicken in a roasting tin or ovenproof dish in which the sweet potatoes and potatoes will also fit in a single layer. Pour half the paste over the chicken and work it in with your hands. Some marinade can go inside the chicken, and you can also lift the skin of the breast (see page 101) and put marinade under that. Cover with foil and put in the fridge for about six hours, turning every so often. Bring it to room temperature before cooking.

Preheat the oven to 180°C/350°F/gas mark 4. Season the chicken, cover it with foil, put it – still in its marinade – into the oven and cook for 30 minutes. Take the dish out and add both types of potatoes to the roasting tin, tossing them in the marinade. Season with salt. Return to the oven to roast for another hour. When there's 45 minutes to go, add the onion, turning it over with the potatoes and juices. When there's 20 minutes left, mix the ingredients for the glaze and spread it over the chicken. Pour the rest of the sherry over the vegetables, stirring, then return to the oven to finish cooking. The chicken should be cooked through and the vegetables tender.

Turn the vegetables over so that they're glossy. Scatter with coriander. This needs cool, fresh accompaniments so an Avocado salsa (see page 82), a green salad and soured cream would be good on the side. Or just add cucumber, avocado and coriander leaves to the salad.

brazilian chicken and prawn xinxim

This is such a good dish, hot and heady with the flavours of South America. You don't actually have to have prawns in it, some versions just have chicken. If you want to leave them out, then increase the amount of chicken by 200g (7oz). But chicken and seafood go really well together, so do try it this way.

SERVES 6

700g (1lb 9oz) skinless boneless
   chicken thighs
juice of 3 limes, plus lime
   wedges to serve
2 tsp cayenne pepper
1½ tbsp sunflower or
   groundnut oil or
   whichever you prefer
salt and pepper
1 large onion, finely chopped
2 red peppers, cut into cubes
3 garlic cloves, crushed
2.5cm (1in) root ginger, peeled
   and grated
3 red chillies, halved, deseeded
   and sliced
250g (9oz) tomatoes, chopped
   (I don't bother to peel or
   deseed)
pinch of soft light brown sugar
300ml (½ pint) chicken stock
2 x 160ml cans of coconut
   cream
300g (10½oz) MSC-certified
   shelled prawns (either tiger
   or king prawns)
10g (¼oz) toasted and roughly
   ground cashew nuts
   (see page 107)
10g (¼oz) toasted, ground
   peanuts (see page 107)
4 tbsp roughly chopped
   coriander leaves
shaved coconut, to serve

Cut each thigh into two or four pieces (smaller thighs – and they do vary a lot in size – should just be halved). Put into a bowl with the juice of two of the limes and the cayenne, cover and marinate in the fridge for about 45 minutes. Bring it to room temperature before cooking.

Heat the oil in a sauté pan, lift the chicken out of the marinade and brown it in batches. You want to get a good colour all over, but not cook the chicken through. Season as you brown the pieces. Remove each batch with a slotted spoon as it is ready and put in a bowl.

Add the onion and peppers to the oil in the pan and cook until these are softening but not brown. It will take about eight minutes. Add the garlic, ginger and chillies and cook for another minute, then add the tomatoes, season, stir everything together and cook for another two minutes. Reduce the heat and cook until the tomatoes are quite soft and slightly losing their shape, about five minutes. Make sure the mixture doesn't get too dry. Add the sugar, pour in 200ml (7fl oz) of the stock and bring to the boil. Reduce the heat to low, cover and cook for 10 minutes.

Return the chicken to the pan with any juices that have run out of it, then stir in the remaining stock and the coconut cream. Bring to a simmer and cook gently for 20 minutes. Stir in the prawns and cook for about three minutes; you will see the prawns turn pink. Stir in the remaining lime juice and the nuts and check for seasoning. This dish can vary in thickness: it can be quite thick; it can be soupy. Add more stock or water if you want it to be more soupy. Sprinkle on the coriander and coconut and serve with boiled rice and lime wedges.

the main attraction *Sunday lunches and posh dinners*

roast chicken with peaches, honey and lavender

A perfect summer dish. It takes little effort and is great to serve in the garden. Don't go mad with the lavender, it will taste sickly if you use too much.

SERVES 4–6

3 tbsp olive oil

sea salt flakes and pepper

1.8kg (4lb) chicken, skin-on, jointed into 8, or 8 good-sized skin-on bone-in chicken thighs

200ml (7fl oz) medium white wine

3 tbsp white balsamic vinegar

4 tbsp lavender honey

5 small, slightly under-ripe peaches

8 sprigs of fresh lavender

Preheat the oven to 190°C/375°F/gas mark 5.

Heat 1 tbsp of the oil in a frying pan, season the chicken joints and brown them on each side so they get a good colour. You can do this in batches.

Put the chicken joints or thighs into a very large, broad, shallow ovenproof dish (both the chicken and the peaches need to be able to lie snugly together in a single layer).

Pour the oil out of the pan but don't clean it. Return it to the heat and deglaze the pan with the wine, scraping to dislodge all the bits of flavour there. Boil this until it has reduced to about 100ml (3½fl oz), than add 1½ tbsp each of the balsamic vinegar and honey. Stir to dissolve the honey, then pour over the chicken.

Halve and pit the peaches and cut each half in two. Dot these in around the chicken. Season with salt and pepper. Brush each piece of peach with a little olive oil, then whisk the remaining honey and balsamic together with a fork. Drizzle this over the chicken and peaches and scatter with the lavender (leave some sprigs of lavender whole, use just the flowers from others).

Roast in the hot oven for 40 minutes. The chicken should be cooked through and glazed with the honey and the peaches should be slightly caramelized in patches. If you stick the tip of a sharp knife into the underside of a thigh, the juice that runs out should be clear. Serve in the dish in which the chicken has cooked (you can transfer it all to a warmed platter if you prefer, but be careful as the peaches will be soft and could easily fall apart). Serve with olive oil-roast potatoes and green beans.

chicken with spring vegetables and herbed cream

This is a plain but luxurious dish that really shows off the best of spring. It isn't difficult, but you need very good ingredients, both chicken and vegetables. It has one drawback: you should ideally use home-made stock, made from raw chicken (get bones and wings from your butcher) not a cooked carcass. It's important that the broth is nice and pale but full of flavour. Stock made from cooked carcasses is darker.

SERVES 6

FOR THE SAUCE

15g (½oz) unsalted butter
1 shallot, very finely chopped
2 tbsp vermouth
1 tsp plain flour
150ml (5fl oz) double cream
juice of ½ lemon
smidgen of Dijon mustard
salt and white pepper
leaves from 4 sprigs of
     tarragon, chopped
2 tbsp finely chopped flat-leaf
     parsley leaves (chervil is
     even better, if you can get it)
3 tbsp crème fraîche

FOR THE CHICKEN

150g (5½oz) peas, podded
     weight
150g (5½oz) broad beans,
     podded weight
18 skinny carrots in a bunch
18 baby leeks
500ml (18fl oz) chicken stock
6 good-quality skinless
     boneless chicken breasts,
     about 175g (6oz) each

For the sauce, melt the butter in a smallish saucepan and gently cook the shallot until soft but not coloured. Add the vermouth and cook until it has almost disappeared. Sprinkle on the flour, stir, then add the cream. Heat to a simmer, then add the lemon juice; the mixture will thicken considerably. Don't panic. Add the mustard, salt and pepper, then add the tarragon, parsley and crème fraîche. The sauce will become thinner when you add the crème fraîche. Check the seasoning, it's really key. Heat through; the herbs will flavour the cream as it heats. Set aside.

Boil the peas and broad beans in separate pans for four minutes. Drain and run cold water over them while they are in the sieve. Once the broad beans are cool, slip the skins off. Trim the green tops from the carrots leaving a couple of cm (about 1in) of greenery. Carefully wash them, especially around the green tufts, to remove any soil. Trim the tops from the leeks, remove any discoloured outer leaves and trim the bases, but leave the bases intact so the leeks don't fall apart. Put the carrots in a steamer or into boiling water and cook until tender. They should be ready in about 15 minutes but can stay in the steamer (or water), covered and off the heat, once they're ready.

Pour the stock into a sauté pan and bring to the boil, then reduce to a very gentle simmer. Add the chicken and poach for 12–13 minutes. Back-time your leeks to be ready with the chicken; steam them for four minutes, until just tender.

Put the peas and beans into boiling water to heat through for a minute. Drain. Quickly reheat the sauce, adding water to let it down. Bring to the boil, then immediately take off the heat.

Put the vegetables – carrots, leeks, broad beans and peas – into broad soup plates. Put the chicken breasts on top, sliced or left whole, and spoon the broth from the chicken round the breasts. You don't want a soup, but the vegetables should be in broth. Spoon some sauce over the chicken and serve.

poussins with black grapes, juniper and saba

Saba – also called vincotto – is grape must. You can buy it online from www.melburyandappleton.co.uk, or in Italian delicatessens. You know those rainy November days we get? Make this. You'll be reminded of what is good about autumn.

SERVES 4

4 poussins
12 juniper berries, lightly crushed
15g (½oz) unsalted butter, slightly softened
salt and pepper
1 large onion, sliced
2 celery sticks, finely chopped
olive oil
600g (1lb 5oz) seedless black grapes, half on their stalks in small bunches, half off their stalks
4 bay leaves
6 sprigs of thyme
250ml (9fl oz) red wine
75ml (2½fl oz) saba

Gently ease the skin off the breasts of the poussins at the cavity openings (see page 101). Mash half of the juniper berries into the butter, season with pepper and gently spread it under the skin (without tearing the skin). Season the birds inside. Preheat the oven to 190°C/375°F/gas mark 5.

Put the onion and celery in an ovenproof dish that will hold the grapes and poussins snugly in a single layer. Season and stir in 2 tbsp of olive oil. Using a wooden spoon (or a mortar and pestle), roughly crush the grapes that are off their stalks so the juice starts to come out. Lay the poussins and the little bunches of grapes on the vegetables and spoon the crushed grapes around them. Tuck in the bay leaves and thyme. Season, sprinkle with the rest of the crushed juniper and drizzle a little olive oil over the grapes and poussins.

Mix the wine with the saba and pour it around the poussins. Put into the hot oven and roast for 45–50 minutes, or until the grapes are slightly shrunken in places and the poussins are cooked. You need to baste the birds every so often. Test they are ready: when pierced with a sharp knife between the thigh and the body, the juices that run out should be clear, with no trace of pink.

Serve, preferably in the dish in which the poussins have been cooked, with buttered cabbage. Spelt, farro or barley, or olive oil-roasted potatoes, are all good on the side.

poussins with indian spices and fresh coriander and coconut chutney

The components here are quite simple, but blend wonderfully together. It's the abundance of the presentation – get out your biggest platter for the poussins – that makes it seem like a feast. Serve with a mango and spinach salad that you've dressed with a nice tart lime and chilli vinaigrette.

SERVES 6

FOR THE POUSSINS

juice of 3 lemons

1 tbsp sunflower oil

4 garlic cloves, crushed

1½ tsp cayenne pepper

¾ tsp ground cinnamon

⅛ tsp ground cloves

pepper

6 poussins

FOR THE BUTTER

50g (1¾oz) unsalted butter

½ tsp ground cinnamon

½ tsp cayenne pepper

2 garlic cloves, crushed

FOR THE CHUTNEY

½ tsp cumin seeds

50g (1¾oz) bunch of coriander, plus more to serve

100g (3½oz) creamed coconut (in a block), or fresh coconut, grated

2 green chillies, deseeded and roughly chopped

3 garlic cloves, roughly chopped

2.5cm (1in) root ginger, peeled and roughly chopped

finely grated zest of 1 lime and juice of 2

salt

3 tsp caster sugar (optional)

To prepare the poussins, mix the first seven ingredients together and rub all over the birds. Gently ease the skin off the breasts and legs of the poussins at the cavity openings (see page 101) and spoon the mixture underneath, too. Place on a large dish, cover loosely with cling film and put in the fridge to marinate for two to four hours. Bring the birds to room temperature before cooking. When you're ready to cook, preheat the oven to 190°C/375°F/gas mark 5.

To make the butter, just mash all the ingredients together in a small bowl. Using your hands, spread this all over the birds, then put them into a roasting tin and cook in the hot oven for 45–50 minutes, or until the birds are a lovely dark brown and, when pierced with a sharp knife between the thigh and the body, the juices that run out are clear, with no trace of pink. Cover with foil and leave to rest for 10–15 minutes.

For the chutney, put the cumin seeds in a dry pan and toast until they are fragrant (about 40 seconds). Put all the ingredients for the chutney into a food processor and whizz to a paste. (If you want a sweet version, add the sugar.) Taste for seasoning. This will be fine in the fridge for three days, but let it come to room temperature before serving, as it sets rather solidly.

To serve, get out your biggest platter. Boil some white basmati rice and stir plenty of chopped coriander through it. Spread the rice out on the platter and put the birds on top. Spoon on the cooking juices – they will make the birds glossy and season the rice, too – and serve with the chutney and a mango and spinach salad.

chicken orvieto

Over the years I have probably cooked this more than any other chicken dish. It's based on a dish in Alastair Little's Italian Kitchen *(out of print but worth tracking down on the internet) and I've changed it only slightly. Alastair Little, who used to have his own restaurant in Soho in London, had a big effect on how we cook… much bigger than he is given credit for. He was the first person, back in the 1980s, to create menus of dishes from the Middle East and Japan as well as Italy, a range that was new to British diners.*

Even though there is fennel in the stuffing, I usually serve this with a creamy fennel gratin – bubbling under a Parmesan crust – and a dish of roast tomatoes. Now that's a great Sunday lunch.

SERVES 6

olive oil
1 large or 2 small fennel
  bulbs, trimmed and finely
  chopped (fronds reserved
  and chopped)
1 small onion, finely chopped
100g (3½oz) pancetta lardons
250g (9oz) chicken livers,
  cleaned and chopped
50 black olives, pitted, half of
  them roughly chopped
finely grated zest of
  ½ unwaxed lemon
leaves from a few sprigs of
  thyme
200g (7oz) waxy potatoes, cut
  into cubes (no need to peel)
salt and pepper
1.8kg (4lb) chicken
50 garlic cloves, unpeeled
250ml (9fl oz) dry white wine
500ml (18fl oz) chicken stock

Heat ½ tbsp of the olive oil in a frying pan and sauté the fennel and onion for a couple of minutes. Add the pancetta and cook until it is golden on all sides and the onion and fennel are soft. Add the livers and toss until they no longer look raw. Put this into a bowl with the chopped olives, lemon zest and thyme. Put 2 tbsp of olive oil into the pan and add the potatoes. Cook until they are tender, stirring occasionally. The potatoes will stick a bit but that's fine. Season. Add to the olive bowl and toss. Leave to cool. Preheat the oven to 200°C/400°F/gas mark 6.

Remove the excess fat around the chicken cavity then stuff the chicken. Either sew up the cavity, or use small skewers. Put the bird in a roasting tin and drizzle some olive oil over it, then rub it all over, including into the space between the legs and body of the bird. Season with pepper and sea salt flakes.

Put into the hot oven and cook for 20 minutes. Reduce the oven temperature to 180°C/350°F/gas mark 4 and cook for another hour. When the chicken has 40 minutes left to cook, toss the garlic cloves into the roasting tin, turning them over in the fat. Check the chicken is done, then put it on a heated platter and cover with foil. Scoop up the garlic, put in a dish and keep warm.

Remove the excess fat from the roasting tin, then set it over a medium heat and add the wine, stirring to scrape up the bits. Boil until about 50ml (2fl oz) is left. Pour in the stock and boil until reduced by three-quarters. Briefly add the whole olives, then strain the cooking juices and add the olives to the garlic.

Cut the chicken into eight joints and serve with the olives and garlic over the top, with any fennel fronds you removed earlier. Put the stuffing on the same platter or into a bowl and pour the juices into a jug. Serve. You don't need any starch on the side.

mustard chicken, black beans and avocado salsa

Hot, spicy chicken, avocado, black beans and cheese too... almost a chicken version of a great chilli. Different, but glorious. Serve with tortillas, soured cream and feta, Wensleydale or mild goat's cheese.

SERVES 6

FOR THE CHICKEN

12 skin-on bone-in chicken
  thighs
125ml (4fl oz) olive oil
60ml (2¼fl oz) cider vinegar
½ tbsp ground cumin
3½ tbsp Dijon mustard
6 tbsp runny honey
4 red chillies, finely chopped
juice of 1 lime
4 garlic cloves, grated
4 tbsp chopped coriander

FOR THE BEANS

2 tbsp olive oil
1 large onion, finely chopped
2 red peppers, chopped
3 garlic cloves, finely chopped
1 tsp ground cumin
2 chillies, deseeded, sliced
finely grated zest of ½ orange
150ml (5fl oz) chicken stock
50ml (2fl oz) orange juice
2 x 400g cans of black beans
juice of ½–1 lime

FOR THE AVOCADO SALSA

250g (9oz) tomatoes
2 garlic cloves
2 spring onions
3 red chillies, deseeded
3 avocados, roughly chopped
1½ tsp ground cumin
juice of ½ lime
4 tbsp chopped coriander
4 tbsp extra virgin olive oil

Make little incisions all over the underside side of the thighs; don't pierce the skin. Make the marinade by mixing everything else in a dish that will hold all the chicken. Put the thighs in, turn, cover with cling film and put in the fridge. Leave for at least four hours – overnight is even better – turning a couple of times. Bring to room temperature before cooking.

When ready to cook, preheat the oven to 190°C/375°F/gas mark 5. Remove the chicken from the marinade and put into a roasting tin or ovenproof dish where it can lie in a single layer. Put into the oven and roast for 35–40 minutes, or until cooked through, basting every so often. The chicken should end up a deep golden colour.

It's really quick to make the beans and salsa, so prepare them while the chicken is cooking. For the beans, heat the olive oil in a saucepan over a medium heat and sauté the onion and peppers together, reducing the heat, until the onion is pale gold and the peppers are beginning to soften. Add the garlic and cook for another minute, then add the cumin, chillies and orange zest and cook for another two minutes. Pour in the stock, orange juice and seasoning and cook over a low heat until the vegetables are soft.

Carefully rinse the black beans and stir into the peppers. Season and heat through for a few minutes. You want the beans to pick up the flavours of the other ingredients; in fact they benefit from sitting in the juices and being reheated at the last minute. Add lime juice to taste, it heightens and freshens the flavours.

To make the salsa, finely chop the tomatoes, garlic, spring onions and chillies. Mix with the other ingredients and season well, but don't make this more than an hour ahead of serving as it discolours. Once you've made it, cover the salsa and let the flavours infuse.

Serve the chicken on a platter with sprigs of coriander, along with the beans, salsa and some cheese and soured cream.

chicken legs in pinot noir with sour cherries and parsnip purée

It's amazing what you can do with some chicken legs and a packet of dried fruit! This dish is dark, rich and rather grand-looking. You don't have to use Pinot Noir, but the grape does have cherry tones. Any other light, fruity red wine is fine, though.

SERVES 4

FOR THE CHICKEN

400ml (14fl oz) Pinot Noir
400ml (14fl oz) chicken stock
4 skin-on bone-in chicken
    legs (drumsticks and thighs
    attached)
salt and pepper
1–2 tbsp olive oil
2 onions, halved, each half cut
    into 4 wedges
3 garlic cloves, crushed
4 tbsp sour cherry juice
    (optional)
4 sprigs of thyme, plus more
    thyme leaves
1 bay leaf
5cm (2in) cinnamon stick
100g (3½oz) dried sour
    cherries

FOR THE PARSNIP PURÉE

500g (1lb 2oz) parsnips,
    chopped
500ml (18fl oz) chicken stock
30g (1oz) unsalted butter
75ml (2½fl oz) double cream
freshly grated nutmeg, to taste
pinch of cayenne pepper, or
    to taste
juice of ½ lemon, or to taste

Reduce the wine and the stock, separately, until they each come to 250ml (9fl oz) of liquid.

Trim the chicken of any raggedy bits of skin and season with salt and pepper. Heat the oil in a sauté pan and brown the chicken legs all over. When they're a good golden colour – and it is really important to get this as it looks and tastes much better in the finished dish – remove them to a plate. Pour all but 1 tbsp fat out of the pan. Add the onions to the pan and cook over a medium-low heat until they are pale gold. Add the garlic and cook for another couple of minutes.

Pour on the reduced stock and wine, the cherry juice (if you've been able to get some), herbs, cinnamon stick and sour cherries. Bring to the boil, then reduce the heat to a very gentle simmer. Return the chicken legs – together with any juices that have run out of them – to the pan. Season, cover and cook for 20 minutes, scooping the wine up over the chicken from time to time. Take the lid off and cook for another 20 minutes.

Put the parsnips in a saucepan, cover with the chicken stock and bring to the boil. Reduce the heat a little and cook until completely tender, about 15 minutes. Strain, reserving the cooking liquor. Put the parsnips in a food processor or blender (a blender produces a smoother purée) and process with all the other ingredients, with just enough of the cooking liquor to make a fine silky purée; remember you are not making a soup, the mixture should be smooth but not too thin. Taste for seasoning and adjust any elements you think are not quite right. Scrape the purée back into the pan and reheat it gently.

The juices in the chicken will have reduced and you should be left with enough sauce just to coat the chicken legs and the fruit. Taste for seasoning and sprinkle on the thyme leaves. Serve the chicken from the sauté pan with the parsnip purée.

paprika roast chicken with caraway potatoes, quick-pickled cucumber and soured cream

I serve paprika chicken with different accompaniments, but think this is my favourite combination. You can also try warm potato salad with chopped sweet-sour cucumber tossed into it, waxy potatoes with sautéed smoked bacon (don't serve soured cream if you use bacon, it's just too rich), and Savoy cabbage with dill instead of the cucumber. It depends on your mood and the time of year. The chicken is also good served with wide egg noodles instead of potatoes (toss the cooked noodles in melted butter and scatter with poppy seeds before serving).

The chicken itself is very simple. But the extra touches – the thyme and garlic inside the cavity, for example – make all the difference.

SERVES 6–8

FOR THE CUCUMBER

1 ridge cucumber, or regular
    cucumber
¾ tbsp sea salt flakes
2 tbsp rice vinegar
3 tbsp caster sugar
2 tbsp chopped dill

FOR THE CHICKEN

30g (1oz) unsalted butter,
    softened
½ tbsp paprika
¼ tsp cayenne pepper
leaves from 4 sprigs of thyme,
    plus 6 whole sprigs of thyme
1.8kg (4lb) chicken
salt and pepper
2 bulbs of garlic, halved
    horizontally
soured cream, to serve

FOR THE POTATOES

400g (14oz) baby waxy
    potatoes
10g (¼oz) unsalted butter
1½ tsp caraway seeds, lightly
    crushed

Cut the ends off the cucumber and slice the rest into very fine slices, they should be almost transparent. Layer in a colander with the salt, place a plate on top and set over a bowl so that the juices can run out. Leave for two hours. Rinse the cucumber and carefully pat dry. Mix the cucumber with the rest of the ingredients and keep, covered, in the fridge until ready to serve.

Preheat the oven to 180°C/350°F/gas mark 4. For the chicken, mix the butter with the paprika, cayenne and the thyme leaves. I usually pound it in a mortar and pestle to make sure all the flavours are mingled well. Put the chicken into a roasting tin and spread the butter all over, rubbing it over the legs as well as the breast. Season with salt and pepper. Put the whole sprigs of thyme and the garlic into the cavity of the bird. Roast in the hot oven for 1 hour 15 minutes, basting from time to time.

The potatoes will take about 20 minutes to cook, so back-time them to be ready when the chicken is done and has rested for about 15 minutes. Boil the potatoes in water until they are tender right through, then drain. Melt the butter in the pan in which they were cooked, add the caraway and cook for about 30 seconds, then return the potatoes and toss with the butter and seeds. Season with salt and pepper.

Serve the chicken with the roasting juices (they're lovely and garlicky as well as full of paprika), a bowl of soured cream sprinkled with cayenne or paprika, the potatoes and cucumber.

how to roast a chicken

There are few things I like better than roast chicken. Crispy, golden, salty skin; sticky brown juices in the pan; a pile of roasted potatoes and a fistful of watercress wilting against its warm flesh… Bliss. When people say they can't ask me to supper because they wouldn't know what to cook (food writers must be the least popular dinner guests), I often say 'Oh, roast chicken and potatoes and a green salad would be great'. And I mean it.

A roast chicken is one of the most basic meals you can cook. Pretty much everyone can do it, but some turn the chicken over, set it on one side and then the other, adjust the temperature, turn the tin round… Some like butter, others swear by olive oil, a few don't believe in any added fat at all. I have sympathy with perfectionists because I have that trait myself, but I need roast chicken to be a simple meal. And I want to vary the ways in which I roast it. Sometimes I fancy butter, sometimes I reach for the olive oil. I might put a lemon inside, or maybe an onion. If I have time, perhaps I'll brine the bird (a great approach, there's a recipe on page 135) or dry-salt it if I can remember to do it the day before (see page 150). So much about cooking is to do with your mood, what you can manage, what's available.

While working on this book I tried many, many different ways of roasting chickens. I cooked them at high temperatures and low temperatures, with different fats, trussed and untrussed, upright, lying on their breasts and even stuck on the central column of an American bundt tin. I tried the different approaches of star cooks: Thomas Keller doesn't use butter (he believes its moisture creates steam that stops a crisp skin forming) though he does give the intelligent instruction 'Roast it until it's done' (I'm not being sarcastic when I mention that). Jamie Oliver wants us to slash the skin on the legs. American food writer Barbara Kafka instructs you to roast your bird fast and high at 260°C/500°F (and do nothing else)… but the resulting bird was dry and my oven smoked like a chimney.

It sounds like a cop-out, but what I found is that there is no 'right' way to roast a chicken. If the chicken has a glaze or marinade that will burn easily (yogurt, crème fraîche, honey or maple syrup) it can't be cooked at too high a temperature. Sometimes I want to add white wine to the tin so I have copious juices, but that means the skin won't be crisp. You make your choices. So you'll find a little variation in the cooking temperatures and methods in this book, depending on the dish.

What I did discover – crucially – is that you need to know your oven. I roasted chickens in friends' ovens and found that the same temperature and roasting time didn't always produce the same results. Anne Willan, in her book *The Observer French Cookery School*, gives her chapter on roasting the title 'By guess and by God'. My mum – who doesn't calculate a roasting time for chicken – says she knows 'by the smell' if a bird is ready. There is wisdom in Willan's title and in my mum's approach, because ovens vary considerably. Mostly I calculate my usual roasting time thus: 15 minutes per 450g (1lb) of weight plus an extra 20 minutes in an oven preheated to 180°C/350°F/gas mark 4 (I do cook it slightly differently if I want very crisp skin, see below).

The other thing that affected my experiments was the quality of the chicken. Generally speaking, more expensive (non-factory-farmed) birds took less time to cook than bog standard (those tended to be 'wetter'). So you have to consider that, too.

We tend to overcook rather than undercook chicken. Check the juices that run out of the bird: they should be clear with no trace of pink. It's better to have to return an undercooked chicken to the oven for a couple more minutes than it is to eat a dry bird.

There are a few more simple rules: don't put a chicken in the oven straight from the fridge, let it come to room temperature first. It's also better to let the chicken sit – uncovered – in the fridge for a couple of hours so the skin dries a bit (no chicken should go into the oven wet). Put the chicken into a tin that fits; if there's too much room round the bird the juices will burn. Preheat the oven (fundamental). If it's difficult to baste with the fat in the tin, use some melted butter instead. Once the chicken is cooked, let it 'rest' for 15 minutes before carving. I make a kind of tent for it from a double layer of foil. To truss or not to truss? I sometimes do when I want the chicken to look neat, or to keep a stuffing in, otherwise I don't bother. Should you put it on a rack in the roasting tin? If you want your bird to be crispy underneath, stick it on a rack. Most of the time I can't find mine and it doesn't bother me (though there are a couple of recipes in the book where a rack is important and you'll see which they are).

When what I want is a plain roast chicken – no stuffing, no adornment, just a golden beauty with a really crisp skin – I buy the best bird I can afford, about 1.8kg (4lb) in weight. I rub 30g (1oz) of butter over the breast and legs and season it inside and out. I put it in a small tin and roast it in an oven preheated to 210°C/410°F/gas mark 6½, the legs pointing towards the back (so the slower cooking legs are in the hotter part of the oven, that is a good habit to get into) for 50 minutes. I don't baste it. I don't move it. While it rests I make a green salad and get out the Dijon mustard. It's perfect every time. And one of the best meals in the world.

spiced roast chicken with barley-pomegranate stuffing and georgian aubergine pkhali

Only the purée here is actually Georgian, but the chicken is inspired by Georgian food. It might seem like a lot of aubergine but when you're only using the insides you don't end up with much purée.

In the summer you can replace the pomegranate seeds in the stuffing with fresh cherries.

SERVES 6–8

FOR THE CHICKEN

80g (2¾oz) pearl barley

1 tbsp olive oil

1 small onion, finely chopped

3 garlic cloves, chopped

salt and pepper

100g (3½oz) feta cheese, crumbled

3 tbsp roughly chopped flat-leaf parsley leaves

3 tbsp roughly chopped coriander leaves

135g (5oz) pomegranate seeds

1.8kg (4lb) chicken

300g (10½oz) crème fraîche

pinch of cayenne pepper

FOR THE AUBERGINES

4 aubergines

olive oil

4 garlic cloves, chopped

1 tsp sea salt flakes

1 tsp ground coriander

1¼ tsp cayenne pepper

good pinch of ground fenugreek

150g (5½oz) walnuts

3 tbsp extra virgin olive oil

4 tbsp chopped flat-leaf parsley leaves

¾ tbsp white wine vinegar

Put the barley in a saucepan and cover with water. Bring to the boil, reduce the heat and simmer for 25 minutes. Drain and place in a mixing bowl. Pour the olive oil into a frying pan and sauté the onion until soft and pale gold, then add the garlic and cook for two minutes. Add to the barley and leave to cool, then add the seasoning, feta, herbs and pomegranate. Check for seasoning. Preheat the oven to 180°C/350°F/gas mark 4.

Brush the aubergines with oil, pierce a few times with a fork, then put them on a baking sheet and roast in the oven for 40–50 minutes; they should be completely tender. Leave to cool.

Remove the excess fat from the chicken cavity. Season the chicken inside, then put it in a roasting tin and stuff. If you want to secure the chicken, you can sew it up with kitchen string, or fix with small skewers. Truss the chicken if you want to. (I often leave the cavity gaping, the stuffing tumbling out, but it's a matter of taste and time.) Mix the crème fraîche with the cayenne and season. Spread all over the chicken, pushing it between the legs and body as well. Roast in the oven for 1 hour 15 minutes; cover the bird with foil if it starts to get too dark.

Put the garlic in a mortar with the salt and grind to a paste. Pound the spices in, too. Add the walnuts, half the virgin oil and half the parsley and pound to a rough paste – I like it with chunks of walnuts – then stir in the rest of the oil, the vinegar, 1 tbsp of water and the rest of the parsley. Taste for seasoning. It will seem really assertive but it works with the aubergine flesh. Split the aubergines in half and scoop the insides into a bowl. Mash to a rough purée, then stir in the walnut mixture.

When the chicken is done the juices between the leg and the breast should run clear, with no trace of pink. Allow to rest for 15 minutes, then serve with the aubergine. You don't really need any more starch, but a bowl of yogurt is a good thing.

lemon and pistachio chicken

I was given this recipe years ago by a chef in a pub in London and have served it every year since, usually around Easter time. I think it's the pistachios that make it; the general greenness and lightness of the dish means it is very right for spring. Serve with spring greens or a big salad of pea shoots and watercress and some sautéed or boiled baby potatoes.

SERVES 6

2 shallots, finely chopped
2 garlic cloves, crushed
leaves from 2 sprigs of thyme
70g (2½oz) unsalted butter
salt and pepper
120g (4¼oz) shelled pistachio nuts
40g (1½oz) white breadcrumbs, plus more if needed
finely grated zest and juice of 2 unwaxed lemons
2 tbsp olive oil, plus more for drizzling
good pinch of caster sugar
handful of flat-leaf parsley leaves, roughly chopped
6 large skin-on boneless chicken breasts
2 tbsp white balsamic vinegar
300ml (½ pint) chicken stock

Put the shallots, garlic and half the thyme into a pan with 50g (1¾oz) of the butter and a pinch of salt. Set over a low heat and cook for five minutes, stirring occasionally. Tip into a large bowl.

Chop the pistachio nuts, or put them in a food processor and blend them until they are coarsely chopped. Add the nuts and the breadcrumbs to the shallot mixture. Add the lemon zest and juice, the oil, sugar and parsley and season well. Stir the mixture. It should form a stiff, coarse paste. If it seems too dry, add a little extra olive oil. If it seems too wet, add extra breadcrumbs. Preheat the oven to 200°C/400°F/gas mark 6.

Place the point of a knife into the thicker side of a chicken breast and cut a cavity that runs along the length of the flesh. Season the breast inside, then, using a teaspoon, fill the hole with the stuffing. Squeeze the sides of the breast together so that the incision closes as much as possible. Repeat with all the chicken breasts. Season the breasts on the outside, drizzle with a little olive oil and put them in a roasting tin. Bake in the hot oven for 20–25 minutes.

Once the chicken is cooked, remove the breasts from the roasting tin and skim off the fat from the juices. Set the roasting tin over a medium heat and splash in the white balsamic vinegar and stock. Bring this to a rolling boil and reduce until slightly thickened. Throw in the remaining butter and thyme and serve the chicken with these juices.

roast chicken stuffed with black pudding and apple and mustard sauce

A good autumnal spin on the roast chicken Sunday lunch. Get good-quality black pudding; I use Clonakilty, though it's not available everywhere. Preparing the sauce ahead makes things easy.

SERVES 6–8

FOR THE STUFFING

25g (scant 1oz) unsalted butter
½ onion, finely chopped
125g (4½oz) black pudding,
    cut into chunks
100g (3½oz) streaky bacon,
    rind removed and chopped
1 small tart eating apple,
    peeled, cored and cut into
    small chunks (you should
    have 125g/4½oz)
100g (3½oz) white or brown
    breadcrumbs
leaves from 4 sprigs of thyme
1 egg, lightly beaten
salt and pepper

FOR THE CHICKEN

2kg (4lb 8oz) chicken
15g (½oz) unsalted butter

FOR THE MUSTARD SAUCE

15g (½oz) unsalted butter
4 shallots, finely chopped
3½ tbsp white wine vinegar
150ml (5fl oz) dry white wine
200ml (7fl oz) double cream
2 tbsp Dijon mustard
squeeze of lemon juice

Start with the stuffing. Melt the butter in a saucepan and sauté the onion, black pudding, bacon and apple together until golden. Mix with all the other stuffing ingredients, season well and leave to cool. Preheat the oven to 180°C/350°F/gas mark 4.

Season the chicken inside, then stuff it and season the outside. Set in a roasting tin and smear butter over the top of the bird. Put in the hot oven and roast for 1 hour 30 minutes. Remove to a warmed platter, cover with a double layer of foil and keep the bird warm. Leave to rest for 15 minutes.

Pour the cooking juices out of the roasting tin and skim off the fat. Pour 150ml (5fl oz) of water into the roasting tin and set it over a medium-high heat. Boil, scraping the base of the roasting tin, until you have about 75ml (2½fl oz) left. Add to the skimmed chicken juices and heat through.

Make the sauce as on page 38, adding the chicken juices. If it is too thick, add water until you get the consistency you want (about that of single cream). Check for seasoning and serve with the chicken, its juices and the stuffing.

cherry and bulgar-stuffed poussins in vine leaves

You can use vine leaves preserved in brine (they come both in packets and jars) if you can't get hold of fresh leaves, but you might find you have them in your own garden (I did, without knowing it), or a neighbour might have them. I first ate this dish in Turkey, where it was made with quail. The Turks certainly know how to make a fuss of cherries.

SERVES 6

FOR THE STUFFING

2 tbsp olive oil

1 onion, very finely chopped

6 garlic cloves, crushed

2 tsp ground cinnamon

1 tsp ground allspice

500g (1lb 2oz) bulgar wheat

200g (7oz) dried sour cherries

800ml (1 pint 7fl oz) chicken stock

400g (14oz) cherries, pitted and halved

large handful of mint leaves, torn

FOR THE POUSSINS

3 tbsp olive oil, plus more for the vine leaves and cherries

6 poussins

salt and pepper

12–18 vine leaves, depending on size, well washed and patted dry

200g (7oz) cherries, unpitted (leave the stalks on, if there are any)

First make the stuffing. Heat the oil in a saucepan and sauté the onion until soft and pale gold. Add the garlic and spices and cook for another minute, then add the bulgar wheat, dried cherries and stock. Bring to the boil, then immediately reduce the heat, cover and simmer for 15 minutes. Add the fresh cherries and mint and leave to cool. Preheat the oven to 190°C/375°F/gas mark 5.

Heat the oil for the poussins in a frying pan and cook them, turning, until golden brown all over. Remove them (and reserve the pan juices). Allow to cool, then season all over and fill them with the stuffing. Brush the vine leaves on both sides with a little olive oil, then place two to three round each bird, tying them with kitchen string. Put into a roasting tin and drizzle with the juices from the frying pan. Season. Cook in the oven for 25 minutes. Toss the whole cherries into the tin and drizzle with oil. Cook for another 20–25 minutes, or until the poussins are cooked through.

Cover with foil and allow to rest for about 10 minutes. Serve on a platter with the cooked cherries. Greek yogurt mixed with chopped mint leaves and a little crushed garlic – and cucumber salad – are good on the side. I like warm flatbread, too.

chicken braised with shallots and chicory on jerusalem artichoke purée

A dish of contrasts – bitter chicory, sweet shallots and nutty Jerusalem artichokes – that comes together very elegantly. I love the colours, too. The palette is completely limited, which gives it a kind of earthy, restrained beauty.

SERVES 4–6

FOR THE CHICKEN

¼ tbsp olive oil

20g (¾oz) unsalted butter

8 skin-on bone-in chicken thighs, or a mixture of joints

salt and pepper

4 heads of chicory (nice fat ones if possible), halved lengthways

16 shallots

250ml (9fl oz) chicken stock

3 sprigs of thyme, plus thyme leaves to serve

FOR THE PURÉE

750g (1lb 10oz) Jerusalem artichokes

good squeeze of lemon juice

225ml (8fl oz) double cream, plus more if needed

50ml (2fl oz) chicken stock, plus more if needed

25g (scant 1oz) unsalted butter

grating of fresh nutmeg

Start with the chicken. Heat the oil and butter in a sauté pan and brown the chicken pieces on all sides, seasoning with salt and pepper. Make sure you don't burn the fat. Remove the chicken and set aside.

Now colour the cut sides of the chicory in the fat as well – you want it tinged with gold – then remove and set this aside, too. Add the shallots to the pan and colour those on the outside as well. Return the chicken to the sauté pan with the shallots and add the stock and sprigs of thyme. Bring to the boil, then immediately reduce the heat to low, cover and simmer very gently for about 20 minutes.

Add the chicory to the pan – try and arrange everything in a single layer – and cook for another 15 minutes. Make sure that there is still stock left in which to cook the chicory. If there is too much liquid, then leave the lid off for the next bit of cooking, so it can reduce. The dish is cooked when the juices in the chicken run clear with no trace of pink and the chicory is completely tender. Taste the cooking liquids: because you have reduced stock, you shouldn't need any more salt.

Meanwhile, to make the purée, cut the Jerusalem artichokes into chunks. I don't bother to peel them, but you can if you want. As you cut them up, immediately drop them in a pan of water to which you have added a good squeeze of lemon juice (this stops the artichokes discolouring). Bring the water to the boil and cook the artichokes until tender.

Drain the artichokes and return them to the pan. Bring to the boil with the cream, stock, butter, nutmeg and seasoning. Heat through, then purée in a blender. Taste for seasoning and judge whether you need to add any more cream or stock (or water) for texture and thickness. Serve with the chicken.

chicken stuffed with courgettes and ricotta

This was inspired by Richard Olney. He has quite a few recipes for chicken with some kind of stuffing under the skin in his classic book Simple French Food *(if you like serious food writing and elegant prose, this should be on your book shelf). One of the joys of a dish such as this is that it needs little else. It already contains vegetables and its own kind of 'embellishment'. A green salad or some roast tomatoes and a grain or bread is all you need with it. Oh, and a bottle of decent wine.*

SERVES 6–8

finely grated zest of
  1 unwaxed lemon
4 garlic cloves, crushed
olive oil
2kg (4lb 8oz) chicken
400g (14oz) courgettes
½ tbsp salt
30g (1oz) unsalted butter
pepper
½ onion, finely chopped
130g (4¾oz) ricotta
40g (1½oz) grated Parmesan
1 egg, lightly beaten
25g (scant 1oz) fresh
  breadcrumbs
leaves from a small bunch
  of basil, chopped

Mix the lemon zest, half the garlic and 3½ tbsp of olive oil together and rub all over the chicken, inside and out. Cover loosely with cling film and leave to marinate in the fridge, turning every so often, for a couple of hours. Bring to room temperature before cooking.

Trim the tops and bottoms from the courgettes, then cut them into julienne strips. Layer them up in a colander, sprinkling with the salt as you do so. Set over a bowl so that the juices can drip out. You really need to do this as you need to dry the courgettes before cooking. Once they've drained for one hour, take handfuls and squeeze out as much moisture as you can, really well.

Melt half the butter in a frying pan and sauté the courgettes for 10 minutes. They should be golden. Season with pepper (you won't need salt) and set aside. Sauté the onion in the rest of the butter in the same pan until soft but not coloured. Add the rest of the garlic and cook for another three minutes or so. Leave the courgettes and the onion mixture to cool completely.

Mash the ricotta in a bowl and add the cooled vegetables, the Parmesan, egg, breadcrumbs and basil. Taste for seasoning. Preheat the oven to 180°C/350°F/gas mark 4.

Carefully loosen the skin of the chicken breast and legs as much as possible, without tearing (see page 101), to create an area you can stuff.

Now take small handfuls of the ricotta mixture and work it in under the skin, pressing the skin on top to spread the stuffing. All the stuffing should go in. Season the outside of the chicken.

Roast in the hot oven for 1½ hours, basting from time to time. Leave to rest – well insulated under a double layer of foil – for 15 minutes before serving.

chicken breasts with wild mushroom sauce and puy lentils

For years this was my 'posh dinner party' number. People used to want a sauce and a bit of cream. Times have changed, but this is still a lovely dish. You can make the sauce and lentils ahead of time and reheat them, which makes it convenient, too.

SERVES 6

FOR THE SAUCE
25g (scant 1oz) dried wild
  mushrooms
15g (½oz) unsalted butter
100g (3½oz) mushrooms,
  roughly chopped
350ml (12fl oz) well-flavoured
  chicken stock
125ml (4fl oz) double cream
salt and pepper

FOR THE CHICKEN
6 skin-on boneless chicken
  breasts (the best you can
  afford), each 150g (5½oz)
20g (¾oz) unsalted butter
a splash of groundnut or
  rapeseed oil

FOR THE LENTILS
2 tbsp olive oil
1 small onion, finely chopped
1 carrot, finely chopped
1 celery stick, finely chopped
300g (10½oz) Puy or Umbrian
  lentils
450ml (16fl oz) chicken stock,
  more if needed (optional)
1 bay leaf
2 tsp sherry vinegar
2 tbsp extra virgin olive oil
1½ tbsp finely chopped
  flat-leaf parsley leaves

Start with the sauce, which you can make in advance if you want and reheat at the last minute. Pour 75ml (2½fl oz) of boiling water over the dried mushrooms and leave to soak for 15 minutes. Melt the butter and sauté the other mushrooms until well coloured. Drain the wild mushrooms, reserving the soaking liquor, and chop any that are large. Add to the mushrooms in the pan and cook for another minute. Pour on the stock and soaking liquor and cook until the liquid has reduced by two-thirds. Add the cream and simmer until the sauce coats the back of a spoon. Taste and season, you shouldn't need any salt because of the reduced chicken stock.

Allow the chicken breasts to come to room temperature.

For the lentils, heat the regular oil in a heavy-based pan and gently sauté the onion, carrot and celery for 10 minutes. Add the lentils, stock and bay leaf and bring to the boil, then reduce the heat to a simmer and cook, covered, for 20–25 minutes, or until the lentils are cooked but still have a little bite. (Keep an eye on them as they turn mushy very quickly.) By the end of the cooking time the stock should have been absorbed (you may need a little more stock or water during cooking). Gently stir in the vinegar, virgin oil and parsley, check for seasoning and cover to keep warm.

Heat the butter and oil for the chicken in a large frying pan. Season the chicken and put it in the pan, skin side down. Cook for two minutes on each side over a medium heat, then reduce the heat and cook for six or so minutes, turning, until cooked through but still moist. Quickly reheat the sauce.

Either leave the breasts whole or cut them, on a slight angle, into two or three pieces. Put some lentils into the centre of six warmed plates, put a chicken breast on top of each serving and spoon some of the sauce around. Serve immediately.

poulet au vinaigre

An old-fashioned classic, this is a lovely main course for a French bistro-style meal. Just make sure – since this requires some last-minute attention – that you have an easy starter and pudding to go either side of it. In fact one of those 'eat-while-you-stand-around' starters (offer saucisson, croûtes with pâté, hard-boiled quail's eggs and tapenade, that kind of thing) is a good idea, so you cook the chicken while you all graze.

SERVES 6

30g (1oz) unsalted butter, plus 50g (1¾oz) more cold butter, cut into little cubes
12 skin-on bone-in chicken joints
3 shallots, finely chopped
6 large garlic cloves, unpeeled
6 tbsp white wine vinegar
325ml (11fl oz) dry white wine
150ml (5fl oz) chicken stock
3 tbsp brandy
3 tsp Dijon mustard
1½ tsp tomato purée
100ml (3½fl oz) double cream
3 large plum tomatoes, skinned and deseeded (see page 150), flesh cut into strips

Melt the 30g (1oz) of butter in a sauté pan and brown the chicken on both sides, skin side first. Add the shallots, the garlic and 2 tbsp of water to the pan and cover. Reduce the heat to low and cook gently for 30–40 minutes, or until the chicken is cooked through but tender.

Take the chicken out but keep it warm (in a low oven, covered). Pour all the fat out of the pan, but don't wash it.

Add the vinegar to the pan, stirring well to dislodge all the sediment that is stuck. Boil quickly until you have about 2 tbsp of liquid left, then stir in the wine, stock, brandy, mustard and tomato purée and mix well. Boil this mixture until you have a sauce consistency.

Press through a sieve into a clean saucepan, pushing the garlic cloves through as well. Add the cream and bring to the boil, then reduce the heat and add the tomatoes. Gently heat through, then take the pan off the heat and gradually whisk in the 50g (1¾oz) of cold butter cubes. The sauce should be glossy. Taste it for tartness; it should be slightly tart but smooth and rounded. Check for seasoning, too. Pour it over the warm chicken and serve immediately.

roast chicken with mushroom and sage butter under the skin

Stuffing a chicken that is to be roasted with butter, just under the skin, is one of the easiest ways you can give it a bit of va va voom and ensure a moist bird, too. The key thing is to lift the skin on the breast very carefully, you mustn't tear it or the butter just runs out.

SERVES 4

15g (½oz) dried wild mushrooms
75g (2¾oz) unsalted butter
250g (9oz) mushrooms, finely chopped
salt and pepper
3 shallots, very finely chopped
2 garlic cloves, crushed
squeeze of lemon juice
6 large sage leaves, finely chopped
1.2kg (2lb 10oz) chicken

Pour some boiling water over the wild mushrooms and leave to soak for 30 minutes. Drain (you can keep the soaking liquid for a mushroom soup or risotto) and chop the mushrooms.

Melt 15g (½oz) of the butter in a frying pan and sauté the fresh mushrooms until they are golden brown and quite dry: mushrooms throw moisture out as they cook and you need this to evaporate. Add the wild mushrooms, stir around and cook for another couple of minutes. Season with salt and pepper. Scrape the mushrooms into a dish and leave to cool completely.

Mix the shallots and garlic in with the mushrooms, add a squeeze of lemon juice and the sage leaves. Now add the remaining butter and mash everything together. Put the butter mixture into the fridge to firm up.

When you're ready to cook, preheat the oven to 180°C/350°F/gas mark 4. Put the chicken into a small roasting tin or ovenproof dish. Loosen the skin of the chicken, starting with the skin on the breast: carefully lift the skin and put your fingers in between the skin and the flesh, working your way down over the skin on the legs, too. You must be careful not to tear the skin. Now push the cold mushroom butter under the skin, spreading it down over the legs. Press the top of the chicken skin once you've used up all the butter, to make sure it is fairly evenly distributed. Season the bird with salt and pepper.

Put the chicken into the hot oven and cook for one hour, basting every so often. Rest for 10 minutes under a double layer of foil. I love this with pumpkin purée – you can fry some more sage leaves and put them on top of the purée – and tagliatelle or orzo, or a brown and wild rice pilaf.

chicken loves herbs

It's hard to think which herbs don't go with chicken. Chicken is often condemned as bland, but can actually stand up to the more robust herbs – such as rosemary, lavender, thyme and sage – as well as being enhanced by the subtler tarragon, parsley, basil, dill, coriander and chervil. If you're doing one of those frenzied post-work shopping trips, throw a bunch of herbs into your basket with some chicken thighs and your supper is already looking brighter. Tarragon is, for many, the star herb with chicken. Those little aniseed leaves can lick their way round a pan of chicken bathed in cream. Or do without the cream and just stick a bruised bunch of tarragon in the chicken cavity.

Or get out the butter. You can stuff herbed butter under the skin, or what about a griddled chicken thigh, dripping with coriander and chilli butter, stuffed into a warm tortilla? That's the kind of supper you want to come home for.

The softer herbs seem comforting with poached or pot-roasted chicken. They create a fragrant breath round the bird: coriander turns your pot of chicken Asian; dill and coriander transport it to the Middle East; parsley brings it home to a British kitchen. Eating chicken bathed in a herby broth makes you feel pure and restored. And it is so simple that it helps you both to taste the chicken and appreciate the flavour of the herb.

Woody herbs can take the fierce heat of roasting. Throwing thyme (and lemon) into the cavity of a chicken is a meal even the laziest cook can muster. A roasting tin full of chicken thighs needs only rosemary and lemon, butter or olive oil, salt, pepper and heat to produce a supper that is more than the sum of its parts.

Lavender shares some of rosemary's qualities and always makes me reach for the honey jar (chicken marinated and roasted with olive oil, lavender, honey and a splash of balsamic is glorious: pure summer). Peaches or apricots are a good addition as their golden flesh shows off lavender's gorgeous purple flowers. Thyme has lovely flowers too but its flavour is more delicate. I've learnt, over the years, not to overwhelm thyme by adding too many other components. And it can always do with a little help. Any dish you cook with thyme (or lemon thyme) needs its flavour 'echoed' by having fresh leaves added at the end of cooking. Sage is, to my mind, slightly brutal, but it does make chicken taste more savoury and seems to bring out a kind of no-nonsense meatiness (offer a side dish of puréed sweet roast pumpkin as a contrast to this and I'm happy).

At least a dozen different herbs are used in this book to produce dishes that range from the delicate to the slap-you-in-the-face robust. Those little supermarket packs of herbs can look rather flattened and powerless. They're anything but. And chicken loves them.

persian chicken with pistachios and mint

I read about a khoresh in Najmieh Batmanglij's wonderful book Food of Life: Ancient Persian and Modern Iranian Cooking and Ceremonies. *It was mostly made from pistachios – a whole 450g (1lb) of them – with the same amount of chicken, no vegetables and a pretty hefty swig of rose water. This is based on that (Batmanglij's recipe also includes verjuice and saffron) but I've messed around with the dish. It uses ingredients I love (and that are common in Moroccan cookery, too), such as saffron and flower water, producing a dish that is scented and unusual to European and American taste buds.*

I have also made this with dill instead of mint and that works very well – it's different, but just as good – while cooked broad beans (whose skins you've slipped off) are a lovely addition, too.

SERVES 4

900g (2lb) skinless boneless chicken thighs
1 tbsp olive oil
2 onions, finely sliced
¾ tsp turmeric
½ tsp pepper
250ml (9fl oz) verjuice
250ml (9fl oz) chicken stock
salt
good pinch of saffron strands
¼–½ tsp rose water (be careful as you are adding this)
250g (9oz) spinach, washed, coarse stalks removed, leaves torn
about 40 mint leaves, torn
50g (1¾oz) pistachios, roughly chopped
rose petals, to serve (optional)

Cut the thighs in half, so that you are left with two pieces that are rough rectangles. Heat the oil in a sauté pan and fry the chicken in batches so it takes a good golden colour on both sides. You don't want to cook the chicken through, just colour it. As the chicken is ready, remove it to a dish.

When all the chicken is done, add the onions to the pan and fry over a medium-low heat until they are golden and starting to soften. Add the turmeric and pepper and cook for another minute, then pour in the verjuice and stock. Bring to the boil, then reduce the heat to a very gentle simmer and return the chicken – and any juices that have run out of it – to the pan.

Season with salt, cover and cook for 25 minutes, removing the lid for the final 10 minutes. Add the saffron, stir it round in the juices to help it dissolve and add the rose water (you don't want to overdo this and different brands have varying strengths, so add carefully and taste as you do so).

Add the spinach gradually, adding each amount when the rest has wilted. Stir in the mint, taste to check for seasoning, then add the pistachios and rose petals (if using). Serve with rice. I also like a bowl of yogurt with some crushed garlic and 1 tbsp of extra virgin olive oil stirred into it.

roast chicken and pumpkin, black lentils and hazelnut picada

Great colours: orange pumpkin, black lentils, tawny hazelnuts, golden chicken skin. Picada *is a Spanish mixture – usually of breadcrumbs, nuts, garlic, herbs and a little liquid – added to a dish towards the end of cooking to thicken it. But lately* picadas *have also been used as a finely chopped mixture of ingredients thrown over a dish at the end to heighten and freshen flavours.*

SERVES 6

FOR THE CHICKEN

1.8kg (4lb) chicken

salt and pepper

6 tbsp olive oil

8 tbsp Amontillado sherry

1kg (2lb 4oz) Crown Prince
    or butternut squash, cut
    into wedges, peeled
    and deseeded

225g (8oz) black lentils

½ small onion, left in one piece

1 celery stick, halved

1 garlic clove

1 bay leaf

2 sprigs of thyme

2 tbsp extra virgin olive oil

juice of ½ lemon

FOR THE PICADA

100ml (3½fl oz) olive oil

30g (1oz) chewy peasant-style
    bread, sliced 1cm (½in) thick

40g (1½oz) skin-on hazelnuts

zest from ½ orange, removed
    with a zester, finely chopped

1 garlic clove

2 tbsp finely chopped flat-leaf
    parsley leaves

1 tbsp sherry vinegar

1 tbsp amontillado sherry

Preheat the oven to 180°C/350°F/gas mark 4. Put the chicken into a roasting tin and season it inside and out. Drizzle with 2 tbsp of the regular oil. Now pour on 4 tbsp of the sherry, both inside and over the top, too. Roast for 1 hour 20 minutes, basting. Put the squash into a roasting tin. Add the rest of the regular oil and season, then turn it over. Drizzle with 2 tbsp of the sherry. Put into the oven after the chicken has been in for 55 minutes (the squash needs to cook for 40 minutes). Allow the chicken to rest for 15 minutes while the pumpkin finishes cooking; it should be tender and caramelized at the edges.

Meanwhile, put the lentils in a pan with the onion, celery, garlic, bay and thyme and cover with water. Bring to the boil, then reduce the heat and simmer for 15–30 minutes, until tender. Keep an eye on them as you do not want mush! Drain and remove the onion, celery, garlic and herbs (if you can find the garlic). Stir in the virgin oil and lemon juice. Season well. Cover and keep warm. (Lentils are fine lukewarm in this dish.)

To make the *picada*, pour the oil into a small frying pan and set over a medium-low heat. Dip a piece of bread in the oil; if it sizzles a bit, reduce the heat slightly and add the bread in a single layer. Fry, turning, until it is a pale caramel colour on both sides. Spread out on kitchen paper and leave to cool.

Toast the nuts in a dry frying pan, stirring, until they give off a nutty smell. Rub in a tea towel while warm to remove skins, then roughly chop. Break the bread into chunks, put in a bag and crush to coarse crumbs with a rolling pin. Finely chop the rest of the ingredients and mix with the vinegar and sherry.

Put the lentils and pumpkin on a large platter with the chicken. Drizzle the chicken with the remaining 2 tbsp of sherry, scatter on the *picada* and serve.

chooks, shoots and leaves *chicken salads*

salad of chicken, cherries and watercress with creamy tarragon dressing

A gloriously summery, elegant salad. You can make this with cold, leftover roast chicken if you prefer – it does mean it's quicker to put together – but it's worth poaching breasts for it, too. Tear the cherries when you pit them rather than cutting them, as the raw edges look better.

SERVES 4

FOR THE SALAD

4 skinless boneless chicken
    breasts
400ml (14fl oz) chicken stock
500g (1lb 2oz) ripe cherries,
    pitted
200g (7oz) watercress
50g (1¾oz) shelled pistachios,
    very roughly chopped

FOR THE DRESSING

1 tbsp white wine vinegar
smidgen of Dijon mustard
salt and pepper
8 tbsp extra virgin olive oil
    (fruity rather than bitter
    or grassy)
2 tbsp double cream
chopped leaves from 5 sprigs
    of tarragon
1½ tsp caster sugar, or to taste

Put the chicken into a saucepan (in which it can lie in a single layer) and cover with the stock. Heat until it just comes to the boil, then reduce the heat until the stock is gently simmering. Allow the chicken to poach in this until it is cooked through, about 12 minutes. (You can check that the chicken is cooked by piercing it with the tip of a very sharp knife, the juices should run clear, with no trace of pink.) Leave the chicken to cool; it stays nice and moist if it sits in its cooking liquor. (The stock isn't needed for this recipe, but keep it for something else.)

To make the dressing, mix the vinegar, mustard and salt and pepper in a cup or small bowl. Whisk in the oil, 1½ tbsp of water and the cream. Add the tarragon and sugar, then mix and taste. You may want to adjust the seasoning or the sweetness. The consistency should be that of single cream. This dressing improves while it sits (the tarragon flavour gets stronger) so cover and leave it to sit for 30 minutes or so.

Drain the chicken and cut it into neat slices – or tear it, if you prefer – and gently toss with the cherries, watercress, pistachios and dressing. Serve straight away.

balinese chicken, bean and coconut salad

The best chicken salads come from the East – Bali, Vietnam, Thailand, Burma – and I can't get enough of them: they just grab your taste buds and don't let go.

You can now buy fresh coconut in small packets (so no more buying a whole beast and taking a hammer to it). I know it's a pain to open a whole can of coconut cream to use just a few tablespoons for the dressing, but there are plenty of other dishes in the book that call for coconut cream, so there should be no shortage of ways to use it up.

SERVES 4

FOR THE SALAD

5 skinless boneless chicken
   thighs
finely grated zest and juice
   of 2 limes
10 garlic cloves, 2 crushed,
   8 finely sliced
salt and pepper
175g (6oz) cucumber
175g (6oz) green beans
150g (5½oz) beansprouts
leaves from a medium bunch
   of coriander, chopped
leaves from a medium bunch
   of mint, torn
125g (4½oz) fresh coconut,
   grated
2 red chillies, deseeded and
   finely sliced
4 kaffir lime leaves, finely
   sliced lengthways
4 shallots
1½ tbsp groundnut oil

FOR THE DRESSING

1½ tbsp caster sugar
juice of 3 limes
2 tbsp fish sauce
1 tbsp groundnut oil
2 tbsp coconut cream

Put the chicken into a dish with the lime zest and juice, the crushed garlic and some pepper. Cover and put in the fridge while you make the rest of the dish. Bring it to room temperature before cooking.

Shave the cucumber skin so that you end up with it in stripes (it doesn't have to be neat). Halve the cucumber lengthways and scoop out the seeds with a teaspoon (discard them). Slice the cucumber as thick as a 50p coin and put into a serving bowl.

Steam or boil the green beans until only just tender (they should be slightly less cooked than you would serve them as a side dish). Rinse in cold water to stop them cooking further. Carefully pat dry with a tea towel. Add to the bowl with the beansprouts, herbs, coconut, chillies and lime leaves.

Peel the shallots, halve them and cut them into moon-shaped wedges. Heat half the oil in a frying pan and cook until crispy and golden. Scoop out on to kitchen paper with a slotted spoon. Add the sliced garlic to the pan and cook until pale gold. Be careful not to burn it; that happens very quickly. Scoop that out, too, on to kitchen paper with a slotted spoon. Add the shallots and garlic to the bowl.

Make the dressing by mixing the caster sugar with the lime juice and fish sauce. Stir vigorously to help the sugar dissolve. Add the oil and coconut cream.

Heat a griddle pan until really hot. Take the chicken out of its marinade and brush on both sides with the remaining oil. Season and cook the chicken on the griddle, starting on a high heat to get a good colour on both sides, then reducing the heat and cooking until they are done. Slice into strips. Toss the chicken into the salad bowl with the dressing and serve.

chicken messina

A chicken version of the classic Italian veal dish vitello tonnato. *You can poach a whole chicken for this instead of breasts, but poaching breasts means the dish is neat and easy to serve. You absolutely must get good canned tuna for it (such as Ortiz). It's a great, easy summer dish and not that well known.*

SERVES 4

TO POACH THE CHICKEN
½ onion
1 celery stick, including the leaves
small handful of sprigs of parsley
6 black peppercorns
4 skinless boneless chicken breasts, about 200g (7oz) each

FOR THE SAUCE
125g (4½oz) mayonnaise, bought or home-made
4 tbsp single cream, plus more if needed
90g (3¼oz) canned tuna, drained of oil and flaked
5 canned anchovy fillets, drained of oil and chopped
1 tbsp capers, rinsed of salt or brine
finely grated zest of 1 unwaxed lemon
salt and pepper

FO SERVE
1½ tbsp finely chopped flat-leaf parsley leaves
lemon wedges

Fill a wide saucepan or sauté pan with water. Add the onion, celery, sprigs of parsley and peppercorns and bring to the boil. Reduce the heat and simmer for 15 minutes.

Add the chicken, making sure that the poaching liquid covers it. Reduce the heat and poach very gently for eight minutes. Take the pan off the heat, cover and leave to stand for 20 minutes. To test whether the chicken is fully cooked, remove one of the breasts and slice it through the middle, cutting it at an angle. It should be firm but moist with no trace of pink. Lift the chicken breasts out of the liquid and put them into a shallow dish. Spoon some of the poaching liquid over them to keep them moist and cover.

For sauce, mix all the ingredients except the salt and pepper. Taste, then season (the anchovies and capers make it salty). It should be spoonable not stiff, so you may need more cream.

Either serve the chicken on separate plates, or on one platter. Slice the chicken breasts across and spoon some tuna sauce on top. Sprinkle with chopped parsley and put lemon wedges alongside. Serve with a lightly dressed watercress and black olive salad (make sure to get good wrinkly olives; you don't need to stone them) and Italian bread.

warm salad of chipotle-griddled chicken, chorizo and quinoa with lime crème fraîche

A wonderful big, sprawling dish, good for a lunch as everything can be served at room temperature. You can extend it by adding black beans to the grains. Offer crumbled cheese – feta or Wensleydale – on the side. Don't be put off by the length of the recipe: the dish is made up of a few components, but each is easy.

SERVES 4

FOR THE CHICKEN

4 skinless boneless chicken
   thighs
2 tbsp olive oil
2 tbsp chipotle paste
juice of 1 lime, plus juice of ½

FOR THE ROAST TOMATOES

8 plum tomatoes
2 tbsp olive oil
½ tbsp balsamic vinegar
1 tsp ground cumin
3 tsp harissa paste
1 tsp caster sugar
salt and pepper

FOR THE REST

200g (7oz) quinoa (mixed
   colours if possible)
2 small avocados
juice of 3 limes
250g (9oz) chorizo
½ tbsp olive oil
25g (1oz) baby spinach leaves
6 spring onions, chopped
15g (½oz) coriander, chopped
½ tbsp white balsamic vinegar
6 tbsp extra virgin olive oil

FOR THE CRÈME FRAÎCHE

200g pot of crème fraîche
finely grated zest of 1 lime

With a very sharp knife, make little slits in the chicken thighs on both sides. Rub with the olive oil, chipotle paste and juice of 1 lime. Cover and leave in the fridge overnight, or for a couple of hours. Bring it to room temperature before cooking.

Preheat the oven to 200°C/400°F/gas mark 6. Halve the tomatoes and put them in a single layer in a small roasting tin. Mix the olive oil, balsamic, cumin and harissa and pour it over. Turn the tomatoes over to coat. Leave cut side up. Sprinkle with the sugar and season. Roast in the oven for 40 minutes, or until caramelized in patches and slightly shrunken.

Toast the quinoa in a dry frying pan for a couple of minutes, then put it into a saucepan and add enough water to cover. Bring to the boil then reduce the heat a little, cover and cook for 15 minutes. Cut the avocados in half and remove the stones. Cut into slices lengthways, then carefully peel the skin off each slice. Season and squeeze over the juice of one of the limes.

Heat a griddle pan until it is really hot and put the chicken on it. Let it sizzle for two minutes. Turn and cook for another two minutes. Reduce the heat and cook until done all the way through, another four or five minutes. Slice and keep warm (just put them back on the griddle and cover). Cut the chorizo into rounds and sauté in the ½ tbsp of olive oil in a pan for about four minutes, until golden brown and cooked through.

Fork the quinoa, season it assertively and put it into a large broad, flat serving dish. Gently mix in the chorizo, chicken, baby spinach, spring onions, coriander, avocado, the juice of the other two limes, the white balsamic and the extra virgin olive oil. Dot the roast tomatoes in among everything else.

For the lime crème fraiche, mix the ingredients with the juice of ½ lime. Serve with the quinoa.

chicken loves citrus

So you're not in the mood for anything complicated, but a smear of butter or a slug of olive oil just isn't quite enough for the bird sitting in your roasting tin. Reach for a lemon. The juice, the zest, the squeezed-out shell you can pop in the cavity… they come in one neat package, bringing a lot of flavour for very little effort. And the lemon's effect is considerable. Its freshness permeates mild-tasting flesh, its juices mix with those of the chicken to produce a sauce in which fat is balanced by acidity. You don't need to make 'gravy', just spoon these citrus-scented juices over the meat.

In the Mediterranean and the Middle East, lemons are the key citrussy flavouring. In South East Asia, it's limes. Limes taste somehow greener, more mouth-puckering, more exotic than lemons. An Indian friend has a great trick. She squeezes lime juice over her chicken and puts halved limes into the cavity – along with a big bunch of mint and peeled garlic cloves – before roasting. The resulting dish is eaten with the cooking juices and rice simmered in coconut milk. This is home cooking that is both down to earth and elevated. And it is the lime – as much as the coconut – which renders it special.

Oranges don't have the astringency of lemons and limes and I use them much less often with chicken, but they produce something softer and sweeter. They're good with warm spices, honey, or a bitter counterpart (try roasting chicken with a mixture of orange juice, honey and ground cinnamon poured over it, basting from time to time, and serve it with caramelized chicory). Oranges are brilliant for their sheer colour too and, because orange flesh can be eaten (without provoking a grimace), they can become an integral part of a chicken dish. Cut thin-skinned oranges into wedges and put them in a roasting tin with poussins. Add olive oil, orange juice, sherry vinegar, seasoning and sprigs of thyme. Sprinkle some soft brown sugar over the oranges and roast. You end up with gorgeous – slightly charred – caramelized oranges to eat with the herby poussin flesh.

Citrus juice isn't just used as an explicit flavouring. A squeeze of lemon or lime juice also works as a seasoning as potent as salt or sugar, a flavour heightener, a connector. When it feels as though an element is missing in a dish – your chicken with tarragon and cream hasn't quite come together, or your pot of chicken and coconut soup tastes somehow 'flat' – the intangible 'something' can often be found in lemon or lime juice. It deepens, rounds out, heightens, pulls the elements of a dish together.

Finally, don't forget lemons and limes when it comes to serving chicken. Citrus wedges aren't just for fish. Other cultures use lemon and lime in the same way we use salt: chicken kebabs, griddled thighs, barbecued poussins, they can all be given a final 'lift' – and a delicious moistness – with a good spritz of juice.

palm sugar-griddled chicken with radishes, cucumber and vermicelli rice noodles

Oh, I love this dish. The cold noodles, the crisp vegetables, the sweet chicken, the heat of the dressing. Try to find watermelon radish, an Asian radish with a stunning pink interior and a great texture. You can use multicoloured radishes (if you can get hold of them) instead, or just regular radishes are fine.

SERVES 4

FOR THE SALAD

1 lemon grass stalk

150ml (5fl oz) soy sauce

50ml (2fl oz) rice wine

40g (1½oz) root ginger, peeled and grated

6 garlic cloves, grated or crushed

4½ tbsp palm sugar or soft light brown sugar

1 bunch of coriander

juice of 2 limes

8 skinless boneless chicken thighs

150g (5½oz) rice vermicelli

175g (6oz) watermelon radish, or regular radishes

150g (5½oz) ridge cucumber, or regular cucumber

2 tbsp groundnut oil

leaves from a small bunch of mint, torn

FOR THE DRESSING

about 2 tbsp raw rice

1 red chilli, halved, deseeded and chopped

2 tbsp palm sugar or soft light brown sugar

2 garlic cloves, chopped

2 tsp grated root ginger

50ml (2fl oz) fish sauce

juice of 1 lime

Remove the coarse outer layers from the lemon grass and trim the top and base. Chop the rest – the softer bit of the lemon grass – as finely as you can. Mix together the soy sauce, rice wine, ginger, garlic, palm sugar, finely chopped coriander stalks, half the lime juice and the lemon grass. Put the chicken in a dish and pour over the marinade, turning to coat. Cover with cling film and put in the fridge for about four hours. Bring it to room temperature before cooking.

To make the dressing, put the rice into a hot frying pan and cook for two or three minutes, shaking regularly, until pale golden brown. Transfer to a large mortar or spice grinder and set aside to cool. Once cool, pulverize. Put the chilli, palm sugar and garlic into a mortar and crush until you almost have a paste. Pound in the root ginger, then gradually add the fish sauce and lime juice and stir in 1 tbsp of the toasted rice.

Put the rice vermicelli into just-boiled water and leave it for four minutes, then drain really well, run cold water through them and leave to drain and cool.

If you have found watermelon radish, peel off the skin then, using a small sharp knife, shave off strips of it in furls. You should end up with something that looks like pink pencil shavings. Or just finely slice regular radishes and the cucumber. Toss the cold noodles with the cucumber, radish, the rest of the lime juice, the oil and most of the mint.

Heat a griddle pan. Shaking the excess marinade off the chicken, cook each piece on the hot griddle on both sides, starting on a medium-high heat to get a good colour, then reducing the heat to cook the chicken through.

Divide the salad between four shallow bowls or one large one. Put the chicken on top and scatter with the rest of the mint. Spoon on a little dressing and offer the rest in a bowl.

smoked chicken, lentil and sautéed jerusalem artichoke salad

This is a bit of a dinner party number – at least that's the way I've often used it – but it also makes a good lunch dish. You can find smoked chicken breasts in larger supermarkets and delicatessens.

SERVES 6

FOR THE VINAIGRETTE

2 tbsp white wine vinegar

1 tsp Dijon mustard

8 tbsp extra virgin olive oil

pinch of caster sugar, to taste

salt and pepper

FOR THE SALAD

3 smoked chicken breasts,
skin removed

350g (12oz) Jerusalem
artichokes, peeled

good squeezes of lemon juice

3 tbsp olive oil

½ onion, very finely chopped

½ celery stick, very finely
chopped

½ small carrot, very finely
chopped

150g (5½oz) Puy lentils

2 tbsp finely chopped flat-leaf
parsley leaves

100ml (3½fl oz) double cream

1 garlic clove, crushed

100g (3½oz) baby salad leaves
(I like baby spinach and
lamb's lettuce)

Make the vinaigrette by simply whisking everything together with a fork. Take the chicken out of the fridge so that it's not fridge-cold when you add it to the salad.

Cook the Jerusalem artichokes in boiling salted water, to which you've added a good squeeze of lemon juice (this stops the artichokes discolouring). Once they're just tender, but still have a little bite (after 10–15 minutes), drain and slice them into rounds about 5mm (¼in) thick. Set aside.

Heat 1 tbsp of the regular oil in a saucepan and gently sauté the onion, celery and carrot until soft but not coloured. Add the lentils and turn them over in the oil. Pour in 500ml (18fl oz) of water, season, bring to the boil, then reduce the heat and simmer, uncovered, until the lentils are just tender. This could take 20–35 minutes depending on the age of the lentils, so keep an eye on them; they can turn to mush very quickly. Drain them. Stir in 2 tbsp of the vinaigrette and the parsley while they are still warm. Heat the cream with the garlic, season with salt and a good squeeze of lemon juice and stir this into the warm lentils, too.

Heat the remaining 2 tbsp of regular oil in a small pan and sauté the artichoke slices until coloured and cooked through. (Be careful not to cook the artichokes so much that they start to fall apart.) Cut the chicken into neat slices.

Toss the salad leaves and the artichoke slices with some of the dressing – don't use it all – and divide between six plates, arranging them in the centre. Spoon the lentils around this and arrange the smoked chicken on top. Drizzle each serving with a little more dressing (you don't have to use it all) and serve immediately, with any remaining dressing on the side.

warm salad of griddled chicken, freekeh, preserved lemon, sour cherries and mint

Even though it's quite summery, you can serve this in the spring and autumn as well. If you're making it in summer you can add some pitted fresh cherries, too. Make sure that the freekeh is well-seasoned and moist: as the grains sit they suck up dressing, so you may need to make some more dressing if it has been sitting for a while.

SERVES 4

FOR THE CHICKEN

4 skinless boneless chicken
    thighs or breasts
4 garlic cloves, grated or
    crushed
salt and pepper
juice of 1 lemon
6 tbsp olive oil

FOR THE SALAD

100g (3½oz) dried sour
    cherries
1 home-made preserved lemon
    (or 2 small commercially
    preserved lemons)
200g (7oz) freekeh
1 tbsp olive oil
4 tbsp extra virgin olive oil
2 tsp honey
3 tsp white balsamic vinegar
juice of ½ lemon
good pinch of ground
    cinnamon
leaves from 10 sprigs of mint,
    torn
10g (¼oz) chopped flat-leaf
    parsley leaves

If you are using breasts and they're particularly thick, cut them in half horizontally. Marinate the chicken if you have time (it really helps). Mix the garlic, seasoning, lemon juice and olive oil in a dish and lay the chicken in it. Turn to coat, cover with cling film and put in the fridge to marinate for a couple of hours. Bring it to room temperature before cooking.

Put the cherries in a small saucepan and add enough water to just cover. Bring to the boil, then remove from the heat and leave to plump up for 30 minutes. Remove the flesh from the preserved lemon and discard, then cut the rind into slivers.

Put the freekeh into a saucepan and cover with water, adding the regular olive oil and seasoning well. Bring to the boil. Reduce the heat and simmer for 25 minutes, or until just tender. Drain. In a small bowl, mix the virgin oil, honey, white balsamic, lemon juice, cinnamon and plenty of salt and pepper. Mix this dressing into the drained freekeh. Drain the cherries and fork them into the grains with the preserved lemon and most of the herbs.

Heat a griddle pan until it is really hot and put the chicken on it (leave the marinade behind). Let it sizzle and splatter and leave it for two minutes. Turn the chicken over and let it cook for another two minutes. Reduce the heat and continue to cook until the chicken is done all the way through, another four or five minutes (it depends whether you are cooking breasts or thighs, breasts cook more quickly).

Taste the freekeh: you might want more lemon juice. The mixture should be moist and well seasoned. Divide between four plates – or put on a platter or a broad shallow bowl – and serve the chicken on top. Scatter the reserved herbs over. I usually offer tzatziki and a green salad on the side.

smoky chicken salad with roast peppers, shiitake and sugar snap peas

The marinating is very important here – it's what gives the chicken its smoky taste – so do it overnight if you can. You can add to or change the vegetables: julienne of carrots, beansprouts and sliced radishes can replace the peppers and mushrooms if you want something lighter.

SERVES 4

FOR THE MARINADE

3 tsp hoisin sauce

85ml (2¾fl oz) soy sauce

85ml (2¾fl oz) dry vermouth

85ml (2¾fl oz) orange juice

½ tsp five spice powder

seeds from 2 cardamom pods, crushed

2 garlic cloves, crushed

strip of orange zest, white pith removed

FOR THE SALAD

4 skinless boneless chicken breasts

2 red peppers

1 tbsp olive oil, plus more to brush

120g (4¼oz) sugar snap peas

16 shiitake mushrooms, halved if large

3 tbsp extra virgin olive oil

good squeeze of lime juice, to taste

about ¼ tsp honey, to taste

150g (5½oz) mixed salad leaves (I like baby spinach and mizuna)

small bunch of coriander (optional)

3 tsp sesame seeds

Mix all the ingredients for the marinade together. Put the chicken in a dish and pour the marinade over. Cover with cling film and put in the fridge for a couple of hours, but ideally 24 hours; this really will improve the flavour. Bring it to room temperature before cooking.

When ready to cook, preheat the oven to 180°C/350°F/gas mark 4. Halve and deseed the peppers and put them into a small roasting tin. Brush with a little of the regular oil and roast them in the hot oven for about 35 minutes, or until tender and blistered. (I have to admit I wouldn't put the oven on just for these, but would cook other things at the same time, such as other roast vegetables for another meal.) Once cooked, cut into slices lengthways. If it looks as though the skin is about to peel off you can remove it. Sometimes I do, sometimes I don't.

Preheat the grill. Lift the chicken out of the marinade and put it on a foil-covered grill rack (the foil just really helps with the washing up). Cook under the hot grill for 12 minutes, six on each side, brushing every so often with the marinade.

Cook the sugar snaps in boiling water for one minute, then drain and run cold water over them. Heat the 1 tbsp of regular oil in a frying pan and quickly sauté the shiitake mushrooms until they are golden.

Reduce the marinade by boiling until it is syrupy. To make the dressing, mix 3 tbsp of the reduced marinade with the 3 tbsp of virgin oil, a good squeeze of lime juice and a little honey (both to taste). Slice the chicken – on the diagonal – and toss with the leaves, the warm dressing, strips of pepper, sugar snaps, shiitake and coriander (if using). Throw on the sesame seeds and serve.

my coronation chicken with mango and avocado

Coronation chicken is the sort of British dish that makes the French laugh (it is, after all, a mixture of meat and fruit, something they find rather alien), but it is one of my favourite things. Usually it looks rather unappetizing, though: you get a pile of mayo-smothered chicken served alongside shreds of iceberg lettuce, all of it scattered with some sad-looking pale almond flakes. I wanted to take Coronation chicken to new heights, to make it into a respectable salad. This is what I came up with. It makes a lovely summer lunch.

SERVES 8 AS A MAIN COURSE SALAD

FOR THE SALAD

salt and pepper

1kg (2lb 4oz) skinless boneless
   chicken breasts, or
   mini fillets

2 tbsp olive oil, plus 2 tbsp
   more to dress the salad

2 just-ripe mangoes

2 ripe avocados

juice of 2 limes

75g (2¾oz) watercress or baby
   spinach leaves

1 red chilli, halved, deseeded
   and shredded

15g (½oz) toasted flaked
   almonds

FOR THE DRESSING

3 tsp curry powder, or to taste

½ tsp ground ginger

350g (12oz) mayonnaise

125g (4½oz) Greek yogurt

7 tbsp mango chutney,
   chopped if it is chunky

a little milk

chilli sauce, to taste (optional)

leaves from 7 sprigs of mint,
   torn

Season the chicken and heat the 2 tbsp of oil in a large frying or sauté pan. Sauté it until golden all over, then throw in about 50ml (2fl oz) of water, cover and let the chicken cook. How long this takes depends on whether you are using breasts or mini fillets; cut one through the middle to check, it should have no trace of pink. Leave to cool completely. Using a fine bladed, really sharp knife, cut into neat slices. Season all over.

Gently mix all the ingredients for the dressing together except the chilli sauce and mint. It should be about the thickness of double cream (though a bit chunky as it has bits of chutney in it). Taste for seasoning and heat and add chilli sauce (if using). Stir in the mint.

Peel the mangoes and cut the 'cheeks' off each side (the bits lying right next to the stones), cutting really close to the stone so you remove the plumpest bit of the mango you can. Cut them into neat slices, about the thickness of a pound coin. (You can remove the rest of the flesh, of course, but it is difficult to cut into neat slices. Best remove it and keep it for something else.)

Halve the avocados, remove the stones and cut the flesh into slices. Carefully peel the skin from each slice. Spoon some lime juice over them to keep them from discolouring. Season. Gently toss the salad leaves with the sliced mango and avocado, the chilli, the remaining lime juice and 2 tbsp of olive oil, salt and pepper (this just gives the salad a nice gloss).

Put the salad on a big platter or a broad shallow bowl and add the chicken. Drizzle some of the dressing over and scatter the almonds on top. Serve the rest of the dressing in a jug. I really like a bowlful of wild and brown rice with this, either warm, or dressed with vinaigrette and left to get to room temperature.

salad of japanese griddled thighs with edamame, sugar snaps and miso dressing

Quite addictive. You can get fresh podded edamame beans in supermarkets now as well as frozen. No need to cook the sugar snaps, by the way; they are gorgeously crunchy and sweet in their raw state. I like the contrast here: hot chicken, cool salad.

The wakame brings a whiff of the seaside, which I love with miso. It reminds me of the Irish seaweed – dulse – that I grew up with. It's entirely optional. I use it dry, crumbled, rather than soaking it.

SERVES 4

FOR THE CHICKEN

75ml (2½fl oz) soy sauce

3 tbsp sake or dry sherry

1 tbsp soft dark brown sugar

4cm (1½in) root ginger, grated

¼–½ tsp chilli flakes, to taste

2 garlic cloves, grated

6 small skinless boneless
  chicken thighs

2 tsp toasted sesame seeds

FOR THE DRESSING

1¼ tbsp white miso paste

2 tsp pickled ginger, shredded,
  plus 2½ tbsp vinegar from
  the jar, or to taste

2½ tbsp groundnut oil

¼ tsp honey, or to taste

2cm (¾in) root ginger, grated

1 garlic clove, grated

FOR THE BEAN SALAD

150g (5½oz) edamame beans

115g (4oz) sugar snaps

8 radishes (mixed colours if
  possible), finely sliced

15g (½oz) micro leaves (such
  as pea shoots, or even little
  sprigs of watercress)

10g (¼oz) wakame, crumbled
  (optional)

Mix together the soy sauce, sake, sugar, ginger, chilli and garlic. Put the chicken into it, turning to coat. Cover loosely with cling film and leave in the fridge for 30 minutes to two hours. Bring it to room temperature before cooking.

Whisk the ingredients for the dressing with 1 tbsp of water, taste for seasoning and sweet-sour balance and set aside.

Cook the edamame beans in boiling water for two minutes, then drain and run cold water through them. Slice the sugar snaps into strips lengthways (this looks lovely, you can see the little peas inside peeking out). Put these in a broad shallow bowl with the radishes.

Lift the chicken out of the marinade, shaking off the excess, and heat a griddle pan. Cook the chicken over a medium heat, turning it frequently, until it is cooked through (this will take about eight minutes). Cut across the thighs into broad strips.

Add the leaves to the salad with the wakame (if using) and toss with most of the dressing. Put the chicken on top and drizzle on the rest of the dressing. Scatter with sesame seeds and serve.

chicken, serrano ham and sherried pear salad with quince dressing

A good salad for autumn and winter. You can find membrillo – quince paste – in delicatessens and at the cheese counter of larger supermarkets.

SERVES 4

FOR THE DRESSING
2 tsp cider vinegar
4 tsp membrillo (quince paste)
salt and pepper
8 tbsp extra virgin olive oil

FOR THE SALAD
3 just-ripe pears
juice of ½ lemon
1½ tbsp olive oil
400g (14oz) chicken mini fillets
10g (¼oz) unsalted butter
2 tbsp medium sherry
160g (5¾oz) watercress leaves, coarse stalks removed
20g (¾oz) blanched hazelnuts, halved and toasted
8 slices of Serrano ham, each torn into 3 pieces lengthways

Make the dressing. Put the vinegar and membrillo into a cup or bowl and blend together with a spoon (you have to use the back of the spoon to squash the membrillo). It doesn't have to be perfectly mixed in. Whisk in the seasoning and virgin oil, using a fork.

Halve and core the pears and cut them into wedges. Squeeze lemon juice on them to stop them going brown.

Heat 1 tbsp of the regular oil in a frying pan and cook the chicken, starting on a medium-high heat so it gets a good colour, then reducing the heat to cook all the way through. Season as you cook them. Remove to a plate. If you think any of the pieces are large, cut them into neat slices.

Heat the butter and remaining regular oil in a clean frying pan and cook the pears over a medium-high heat initially – you want the pear flesh to get a good colour – then reduce the heat and cook until tender (be careful not to burn the butter). Quickly add the sherry and cook until it has coated the pears well and bubbled away to almost nothing. The pears should really become imbued with the sherry and turn quite dark in colour.

Quickly toss the leaves, nuts, ham and chicken together with most of the dressing. Arrange on plates and divide the pieces of pear between them. Drizzle on the remaining dressing and serve.

chicken, asparagus, broad bean and radish salad with dill and mint dressing

Very elegant and light, a perfect lunch salad and a dazzling mixture of pink, purple and green (especially if you can find a mixture of different coloured radishes). When asparagus isn't in season, use green beans or sugar snap peas instead.

SERVES 4

FOR THE SALAD

400ml (14fl oz) chicken stock

4 skinless boneless chicken breasts, about 175g (6oz) each

135g (5oz) watermelon radish (or regular radishes, or a mixture)

300g (10½oz) broad beans

16 asparagus stalks, halved lengthways

FOR THE DRESSING

2 tbsp white balsamic vinegar

½ tsp Dijon mustard

8 tbsp extra virgin olive oil (fruity rather than grassy)

salt and pepper

4 tbsp double cream

½ tbsp chopped dill

½ tbsp chopped mint leaves

Put the stock into a sauté pan or a wide saucepan in which the chicken breasts can lie without touching each other. Bring to the boil, reduce the heat to a very gentle simmer and put the chicken into it. Poach for 12–13 minutes. This should give you meat that is cooked but still moist. You can serve the chicken warm or at room temperature. (The stock isn't needed for this recipe, but keep it for something else.)

Slice the radishes into thin rounds (if you have found watermelon radish, see page 118 for how to prepare it).

Make the dressing by putting the vinegar and mustard into a cup or bowl and then whisking in the olive oil, seasoning, cream and herbs. Set aside.

Boil the broad beans for four minutes. Drain and run cold water over them while they are in the sieve. Once the broad beans are cool, slip the skin off each one (it's laborious but worth it for the colour).

Steam the asparagus, or cook it in a covered saucepan with the base of the stalks in a little water and the rest propped up against the side (unless you have an asparagus steamer). The asparagus should still have a little 'bite'; check it with the tip of a sharp knife.

Cut each chicken breast on the diagonal into about four slices. Toss the broad beans, radishes and asparagus with half the dressing. Divide between four plates. Put the chicken on top and spoon on the rest of the dressing. If there's some dressing left over, offer it at the table.

mexican griddled chicken, sweet potato and avocado salad with chipotle mayo

Another South American-inspired dish. You can buy chipotle paste in jars nowadays, very useful for both dressings and marinades. If you don't like quinoa you can use brown rice instead, or a mixture of brown and wild rices. And if you don't want to make the mayo yourself, use a good commercial variety, adding lime juice, chipotle paste and soured cream.

SERVES 4–6

FOR THE CHICKEN

4 skinless boneless chicken
  thighs
4 garlic cloves, grated
juice of 1 lime
4 tbsp olive oil, plus more for
  the sweet potatoes
½ tsp ground cumin
450g (1lb) sweet potatoes,
  peeled
salt and pepper
150g (5½oz) quinoa (a mixture
  of red and white is good)
1 tbsp white balsamic
3 tbsp extra virgin olive oil
½ tsp cumin seeds
¼ tsp dried chilli flakes
1 ripe avocado
100g (3½oz) baby spinach
small bunch of coriander
  (about 15g/½oz)

FOR THE MAYONNAISE

1 egg yolk
½ tsp Dijon mustard
150ml (5fl oz) mixed olive and
  groundnut or sunflower oil
5 tsp chipotle paste
½ tsp soft light brown sugar
juice of ½ lime
1 tbsp soured cream

Put the thighs into a dish and add the garlic, lime juice, regular oil and ground cumin. Turn the chicken to coat. Cover with cling film and marinate in the fridge for two to four hours. Bring it to room temperature before cooking.

Preheat the oven to 200°C/400°F/gas mark 6. Cut the sweet potatoes into slices about 1.5cm (⅔in) thick. Brush on both sides with regular oil and season. Put on a baking sheet and bake for 20 minutes, until just soft and golden, turning halfway.

To make the mayonnaise, mix the egg yolk and mustard in a bowl. Beating constantly with an electric beater, pour in the oils, a very little at a time. Stir in the chipotle paste, sugar, lime juice, seasoning and soured cream, adding 1 tbsp of water.

Cook the quinoa (see page 114). Tip into a broad, shallow serving bowl, season and add the white balsamic and virgin oil.

Heat a griddle pan and cook the sweet potatoes for two minutes on each side, to get a smoky flavour and nice griddle marks. Press the slices to encourage the marks to form. Sprinkle with cumin seeds and chilli flakes as you are cooking.

Add the sweet potato to the quinoa. Lift the chicken out of its marinade – shaking off the excess – and cook it on the griddle pan set over a medium-high heat for about two minutes on each side. Reduce the heat a little and cook for five minutes, turning from time to time. It should be cooked through.

Halve the avocado, pit and cut into slices, then carefully remove the skin from each slice. Add the avocado to the quinoa with the spinach and coriander. Toss carefully and check the whole thing for seasoning. Slice the chicken into broad strips and put it on top. Drizzle with the mayonnaise – don't use too much, you can offer the rest on the side – and serve.

chicken, bacon and potato salad with buttermilk and herb dressing

An easy American-style salad (they do love a buttermilk dressing). You can add sliced avocado and halved cherry tomatoes if you want and I sometimes add chopped cornichons to the dressing.

SERVES 6

FOR THE DRESSING
375ml (13fl oz) buttermilk
6 tbsp double cream
1 garlic clove, crushed
4 spring onions, finely sliced
2 tbsp chervil leaves (or parsley leaves if you can't find chervil), finely chopped
salt and pepper

FOR THE SALAD
500g (1lb 2oz) baby waxy potatoes
10g (¼oz) unsalted butter
4 skinless boneless chicken breasts
3½ tbsp olive oil
200g (7oz) green beans, topped
9 thick rashers of good-quality streaky bacon (smoked or unsmoked)
300g (10½oz) cos lettuce, leaves separated and torn

For the dressing, mix everything together, season well and put it in the fridge until you need it.

Try to cook everything else so that all the ingredients are still warm at the same time. Boil the potatoes until tender, drain, return to the pan, add the butter, season and cover until needed.

If the chicken breasts are particularly thick, cut them in half horizontally. Using 2 tbsp of the oil, brush them on each side and season. Heat a griddle pan until hot and cook the chicken for about three minutes, turning once (and moving the chicken round the griddle so that no pieces are cooking in the cooler patches). Season. Reduce the heat and cook for another two minutes, or until the chicken is cooked through (but not overcooked, it should still be moist).

Steam the beans over boiling water until al dente and fry the bacon in the remaining oil until just crisp, then cut each rasher in half.

Cut the chicken breasts – at an angle – into broad slices. Halve the potatoes and gently toss them, the lettuce and the beans together with a little of the buttermilk dressing, then put the chicken and bacon on top and drizzle over the rest of the dressing. Serve immediately.

feast *let's celebrate*

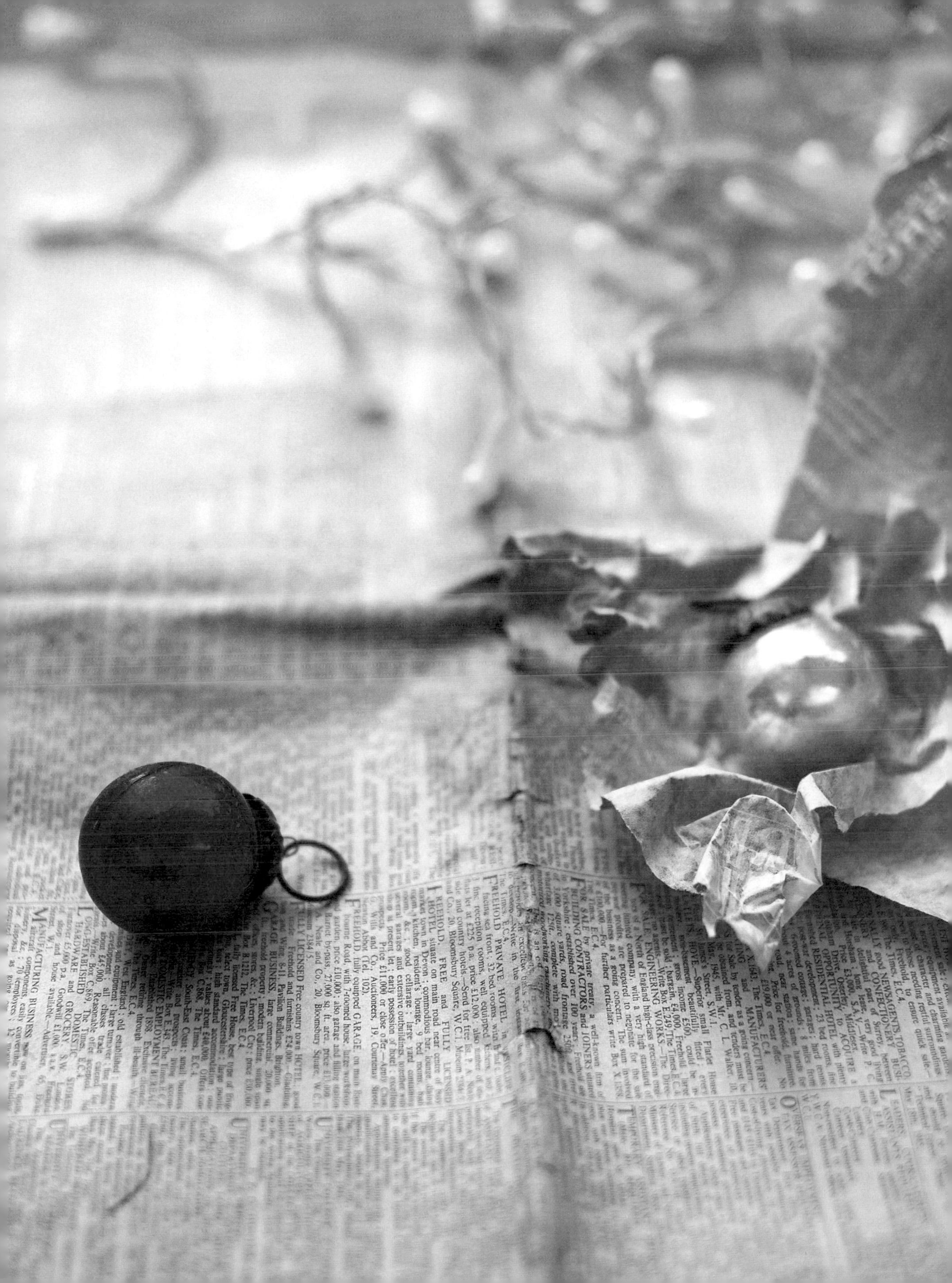

cider-brined chicken with prunes, chestnuts and baby onions

An excellent Christmas option if you don't want to cook a turkey. It's as bronze as a footballer's WAG (the brine, because it contains sugar, means that the skin becomes a good deep colour) and looks glorious.

Some farmers produce really big chickens for Christmas and Easter: Fosse Meadows have them, while SJ Fredericks do Label Anglais chickens that weigh as much as 3.5kg (7lb 10oz) especially for these times of year, so you could opt for a really big chicken instead of a turkey.

Brining may seem like a hassle, but I'm a bit of a convert. It really does season the meat right through to the bone – providing a conduit for all manner of flavours, too – and ensures moistness. The only troublesome thing is finding a cold place where you can brine your chook for 24 hours. It usually means taking the veg drawer out of the fridge, but you may have a very cold room in the house. It's important that you don't brine the chicken for any longer than suggested, or it will be too salty.

Be careful with the prune dish. The prunes must be soft and tender, but not collapsing into a chutney. You need to use heat judiciously.

SERVES 8

FOR THE BRINE

125g (4½oz) sea salt flakes

1 tbsp black peppercorns

1½ tbsp juniper berries

2 tbsp allspice berries

300ml (½ pint) maple syrup

75g (2¾oz) soft light brown sugar

8 sprigs of thyme

4 bay leaves

1 litre (1¾ pints) dry cider

2.5kg (5lb 8oz) chicken

TO SOAK THE PRUNES

30 plump Agen prunes

200ml (7fl oz) apple brandy

½ tbsp granulated sugar

To make the brine, put all the ingredients into a very large saucepan with 3 litres (5¼ pints) of water. Gently heat, stirring to help the salt and sugar dissolve, until boiling. Leave to cool completely. Put this into a scrupulously clean bucket or other large plastic container. (Remember the level of the liquid will rise after you put in the chicken, so make sure there's enough room.) Put in the chicken and weigh it down with a plate (you may need something else too, a bottle of vodka does the trick). Leave somewhere cold for 24 hours. Unless there's snow on the ground – that's when one of the rooms in my house gets very cold – I take the veg drawers out of the fridge and put it there.

Start the prunes the day before, too, if possible. Put them into a saucepan with 200ml (7fl oz) of the apple brandy, the sugar and 100ml (3½fl oz) of water. Bring to the boil, then reduce the heat and simmer until the prunes are soft and plump and most of the liquid has been absorbed, about 15 minutes. This is best done the day before so they have time to plump up, but you can do it early in the day on which you want to serve the chicken.

After 24 hours, take the chicken out of the brine and dry it thoroughly with kitchen paper. Leave it to dry in the fridge – uncovered – for a couple of hours, then bring it to room temperature. Preheat the oven to 180°C/350°F/gas mark 4.

continued...

handful of parsley stalks
1 orange, halved
1 onion, halved
150ml (5fl oz) dry cider
600ml (1 pint) well-flavoured
    chicken stock

TO FINISH THE PRUNES
15g (½oz) unsalted butter
20 baby onions, peeled
100ml (3½fl oz) apple brandy
200ml (7fl oz) chicken stock
2 sprigs of thyme
20 cooked chestnuts
1 tsp sherry vinegar

Put the chicken into a roasting tin and put the parsley stalks, orange and onion inside the cavity. Roast for 1 hour 40 minutes, basting every so often. (Because of the sugar in the brine the skin can darken quite quickly. If it gets too dark, cover the chicken with foil.)

The chicken is ready when the juices that run out from between the leg and the body are clear, with no trace of pink. Pour the juices off into a heatproof glass jug and put the bird on to a heated platter. Cover with a double layer of foil and let the chicken rest for 15 minutes.

Skim the fat from the chicken roasting juices. Make a 'gravy' by deglazing the roasting tin with the cider: add the cider and bring to the boil while stirring with a wooden spoon to dislodge all the bits stuck to the bottom of the tin. Reduce the alcohol by half, add the chicken stock and the skimmed chicken juices and boil until you have a light syrup.

While all this is going on, finish the prunes. Heat most of the butter in a frying pan and sauté the onions until golden all over, about 10 minutes. Be careful not to burn the fat. Add the apple brandy and boil until only about 4 tbsp of liquid remains. Add the chicken stock and thyme to the onions, bring to the boil, then reduce the heat to a simmer. Cook, covered, for about 10 minutes, then remove the lid and continue to cook until the onions are tender and the liquid has really reduced. Remove the thyme. Melt the last bit of butter in another frying pan and quickly sauté the chestnuts until they are glossy. Add these and the onions to the prunes and stir in the sherry vinegar. Heat everything through, but don't boil the mixture or the prunes will start to fall apart; you don't want a chutney. Taste for seasoning. There should be a touch of sweet-savoury going on but the dish shouldn't be too sweet.

Either serve the prune, onions and chestnuts in a bowl, or spoon them round the bird on its platter. Offer the reduced cooking juices in a warmed jug. Of course, it goes with all the usual Christmas razzamatazz of side dishes.

a bird at the feast

I love all the recipes in this book – otherwise they wouldn't be here – but I was really struck, when cooking the dishes for this Feast chapter, just how well a chicken can step up to the mark. We tend to take it for granted now, but chicken hasn't always been seen as 'everyday' fodder. In the past it was seen as special and expensive and chicken 'feast' dishes evolved in many cultures. In Catalonia, *mar i muntanya*, a braise of chicken, prawns, almonds, tomatoes and a little anisette, was considered a very special dish not because of the prawns – which were plentiful – but because of the chicken, which took time and money to grow. The original blancmange (or *biancomangiare*), a celebrated dish of medieval cuisine, was made from rice flour, sugar, rose water, almond milk and pounded chicken breast (a version of this – tavuk göğsü – still survives in modern Turkey). Chicken was used for it because of the paleness of its meat. *The Oxford Companion to Italian Food* says that *biancomangiare* was revered because of 'its unearthly and expensive whiteness' and that the dish 'spoke of conspicuous consumption and a flagrant use of costly commodities'. Elizabeth Ayrton writes about Gervase Markham's Chicken Pye from 1615, a splendid creation rich with chicken, currants, raisins, cinnamon, sugar, mace and flower water. A dull old bird? Not always.

I think it's possible for chicken, even these days when it's ubiquitous, to have status as well as being a 'go-to' food. For the recipes in this chapter, buy the very best bird you can afford; you'll notice the difference. A really good chicken will cost a bit (and taste particularly good) and it's worth it for special meals; I fork out for a really good chicken much more often than I used to. The sight of a whole bronzed bird makes people sigh – it is at once comforting and elevated – and it's hard to devalue that. I'd like to reclaim chicken as the central focus of the feast.

The meals that follow aren't just dictated by the calendar (Christmas, Jewish New Year or Valentine's Day), they're for get-togethers that are simply a bit more celebratory than a regular Sunday lunch. There are big sprawling dishes – Lebanese fatteh, for example, moist chicken layered up with rice, tomato sauce, golden aubergines, herbs and pomegranates; a little bollito misto, a baby version of the great Italian dish – that are great for feeding a crowd. There are also 'feasts' for two or four people, meals that aren't big in a physical sense but that are special because they're designed to mark some important event. For these, you can justify spending money on truffles or a bottle of obscure wine from the Jura to embellish your bird. A feast doesn't have to be big: two people can feast on the joyous luxury of a bird with truffles stuffed under its skin.

So plan a gathering, large or small and put chicken in the middle of the table. Honour that bird. Feast.

crusted chicken and chorizo paella

I've made lots of paellas in my time, they're very low maintenance (as you actually must leave them to cook, not stir them) and they're good for a crowd. But I only recently made this one with an egg crust. Why did I wait so long? It adds another layer of texture and flavour and softens and enriches the whole dish. Just make sure to get a nice soft set.

SERVES 6–8

1 litre (1¾ pints) chicken stock
¼ tsp saffron strands
3 tbsp olive oil
salt and pepper
8 skin-on bone-in chicken
    thighs
250g (9oz) spicy sausages, cut
    into chunks
150g (5½oz) chorizo sausage,
    cut into chunks
1 large onion, roughly
    chopped
4 garlic cloves, crushed
400g (14oz) tomatoes, chopped
3 tsp smoked paprika
1 tsp chilli flakes
375g (13oz) Spanish paella rice
325g jar of roasted peppers
    (or 4 home-roasted peppers),
    drained and sliced
5 medium eggs
1 tbsp chopped flat-leaf
    parsley leaves
finely grated zest of ½
    unwaxed lemon
generous grating of nutmeg
lemon wedges, to serve

Bring the stock to the boil in a medium saucepan. Stir in the saffron, remove the pan from the heat and set aside.

Heat 1 tbsp of the oil in a paella pan, large deep frying pan or broad shallow casserole (I use a cast-iron one for this) that is at least 30cm (12in) in diameter. Season the chicken thighs and brown them on both sides. (You want to colour the chicken well, not cook it through.) Take the chicken out of the pan and set it aside. Add the sausages and chorizo to the pan and brown all over, then set aside with the chicken.

Pour off all but 1½ tbsp of fat from the pan. Add the onion and cook until it is soft and golden, about four minutes, then add the garlic and cook for another two minutes. Add the tomatoes and cook for another four minutes. Stir in the paprika and chilli and cook for a minute, stirring, then add the chicken stock. Return the chicken, sausages and chorizo, bring to a simmer and cook over a gentle heat for 10 minutes.

Pour the rice all round the chicken and season everything really well. Cook for 25 minutes. You don't need to stir the rice as it cooks, in fact you shouldn't.

Ten minutes before the end of cooking time add the peppers, tucking them in among the meat and rice. When the cooking time is up, all the stock should have been absorbed. Preheat the oven to 220°C/425°F/gas mark 7 or preheat the grill to its highest setting to coincide with the end of the cooking time.

Meanwhile, lightly beat the eggs in a bowl with some salt, pepper, the parsley, lemon zest and nutmeg. Pour this over the top of the paella, tilting the pan from side to side to ensure an even layer of egg (if it seeps into the paella rather than making a crust on top it just produces a heavy dish). Now either put the dish in the hot oven or under the hot grill for five minutes. The top should be set and crusty. Serve with lemon wedges.

jura chicken with vin jaune and morels

The reason this gets a place in the feasting chapter is that it's expensive to make and the ingredients are hard to find. It takes effort, but it's one of the most glorious French dishes I know and well worth it for a special meal. Morels are in season in the spring. If you can't get hold of fresh morels, or prefer not to splash out, dried wild morels are fine (more than fine, in fact!) Buy the best chicken you can afford.

In the Jura region of France they produce a strange dry white wine called vin jaune. *It's difficult to find here, but dry sherry is a good substitute.*

SERVES 6

300g (10½oz) fresh morel
    mushrooms (or a mixture
    of morels and cultivated
    mushrooms), or 40g (1½oz)
    dried morel mushrooms
75g (2¾oz) unsalted butter
1.8kg (4lb) skin-on chicken,
    jointed into 8
salt and pepper
300ml (½ pint) *vin jaune* or
    dry sherry
200ml (7fl oz) double cream
juice of ½ lemon, or to taste
    (optional)
chopped chervil leaves (if you
    can find it) to serve, or
    finely chopped flat-leaf
    parsley leaves

If you are using fresh mushrooms, gently clean them (if you have a little brush that's great, otherwise go carefully with kitchen paper). If you are using dried mushrooms, put them in a bowl and add enough just-boiled water to cover. Leave these to soak for 30 minutes.

Heat half the butter in a sauté pan and, working in batches, brown the chicken over a medium heat. Be careful not to burn the fat. Season. Remove the chicken to a dish as each piece is ready and set aside while you work on the others.

Add the remaining butter to the pan with the mushrooms (drain if you're using dried mushrooms and keep the soaking liquor) and sauté briskly for five minutes. Add the wine, stirring to dislodge all the lovely juices that have stuck to the pan and bring to the boil. If you have soaking liquor from dried mushrooms, add that too, avoiding any gritty bits at the bottom of the bowl. Return the chicken to the pan, reduce the heat to low, cover and cook gently for about 40 minutes, or until cooked through. Take out the chicken pieces and put them in a dish in a low oven while you make the sauce.

Skim excess fat from the top of the cooking liquor. Bring the cooking liquor to the boil and reduce by about one-quarter. Add the cream and return to the boil. Cook until you have a sauce that will just coat the back of a spoon, not too thick and not too thin. Taste for seasoning.

Sometimes the elements of a dish can be 'lifted' by a squeeze of lemon juice so add this if you think it needs it; the lemon will also thicken the sauce slightly. Taste again for seasoning. Return the chicken to the pan and heat it through. Scatter the chervil or parsley on top and serve from the sauté pan.

greek chicken with greens, capers and skordalia

Chicken with potatoes, oregano and lemon is a Greek classic and a brilliant Sunday lunch dish. This is just a little more special, and perfect for an Easter feast. Skordalia is a garlic sauce based on potatoes, bread or nuts. This one is half bread and half nuts, as I liked the idea of serving roast chicken and potatoes with a bread sauce (as we do in Britain)... but of a very different kind.

One last thing: your stock should be pale. If you use a dark stock, the potatoes end up pretty brown in colour. It still tastes good but doesn't look quite as nice.

SERVES 8

FOR THE CHICKEN

4 garlic cloves
sea salt flakes and pepper
1½ tbsp dried wild oregano
8 tbsp extra virgin olive oil
juice of 2 lemons
1.8kg (4lb) chicken
1.2kg (2lb 10oz) waxy potatoes,
    peeled and quartered
300ml (½ pint) light chicken
    stock
350g (12oz) spinach leaves,
    coarse stalks removed, torn
150g (5½oz) frisee leaves (also
    known as curly endive), use
    the paler leaves, torn
3 tbsp capers, rinsed

FOR THE SKORDALIA

75g (2¾oz) coarse white bread,
    without crusts
6 garlic cloves, chopped
½ tsp sea salt flakes
75g (2¾oz) pine nuts, toasted
200ml (7fl oz) extra virgin
    olive oil
2–4 tbsp red wine vinegar

Start with the chicken. Put the garlic in a mortar with some sea salt and pepper and crush to a paste. Add the oregano and pound again, then 5 tbsp of the olive oil and half the lemon juice. Put the chicken in a roasting tin in which the potatoes will fit as well and rub the mixture over it, especially on the breast. Cover with cling film and put in the fridge for a couple of hours. Bring it to room temperature before cooking.

When ready to cook, preheat the oven to 180°C/350°F/gas mark 4. Put the potatoes in the tin around the chicken, drizzle with the remaining olive oil and lemon juice and season. Heat the stock and pour it over. Roast for 1 hour 20 minutes, basting.

Make the *skordalia*. Put the bread in a bowl. Sprinkle with 100ml (3½fl oz) of water and leave to soak, then squeeze the water from the bread. Put the garlic into a mortar with the salt and grind to a paste. Pound in the bread, then the nuts (it's hard, but gives a better texture than the food processor, though use that if you prefer). Add the oil gradually, pounding and mixing after each addition, then add the vinegar to taste and pepper. It should be like bread sauce. If it's too thick, add a little hot water and taste in case you need to adjust the seasoning.

When the chicken is cooked, lift it on to a heated platter, cover with foil and rest for 15 minutes.

Set the roasting tin over a medium heat. If there is a lot of liquid, boil so it evaporates, stirring the potatoes (try not to break them up; be gentle). Add the spinach and frisee and turn with the potatoes so they wilt. The frisee won't wilt very much, that's fine. Toss the capers in and taste for seasoning.

Put the potatoes and greens round the chicken on its platter and serve with the *skordalia* on the side.

little (ish) bollito misto

One of the classics of Italian food, this dish from Piedmont is a wonderful old-fashioned feast. A proper big bollito feeds about 18 and includes tongue and sometimes veal. It seems a pity only to cook it when you have hordes to feed, so this is a reduced version. Buy good brisket from an excellent butcher – one from the supermarket won't do – and cook it really gently, or the meat will be tough. You can find cotechino and mostarda di frutta *in Italian delis or online.*

SERVES 10

FOR THE BOLLITO MISTO

500g (1lb 2oz) beef bones

3 carrots

3 celery sticks

2 leeks, cleaned, trimmed
   and halved

1 large onion, peeled, halved,
   each half stuck with 1 clove

generous handful of parsley
   stalks

10 black peppercorns

1kg (2lb 4oz) beef brisket

sea salt flakes

1 small chicken

1 cotechino

FOR THE SALSA VERDE

100g (3½oz) flat-leaf parsley
   sprigs

25g (scant 1oz) mint leaves

2 garlic cloves, chopped

2 tbsp capers, rinsed

4 anchovies, rinsed, dried
   and chopped

½ tsp Dijon mustard

juice of ½ lemon

freshly ground black pepper

150ml (5fl oz) extra virgin
   olive oil

Put the beef bones, carrots, celery, leeks, onion, parsley stalks and peppercorns into a very large saucepan (it needs to hold the beef and the chicken at the same time). Add cold water to cover and bring to the boil. Skim the surface, reduce the heat to a simmer and cook for 1½ hours. Add the brisket, return to just under the boil, then reduce to a gentle simmer. Skim the surface and add salt. Cover and cook very, very gently for 1 hour 15 minutes. Add the chicken and cook for another 45 minutes. The chicken should be cooked through (the juices that run from between the leg and the body should be clear, with no trace of pink). Make sure the cooking is gentle the whole time.

To make the salsa verde, chop the herbs, then pound in a mortar and pestle with the other ingredients, gradually adding the oil (you can make this in the food processor, but it is nicer made by hand: it has a better, rougher texture). Some cooks add the yolks of two hard-boiled eggs, to enrich and soften the salsa.

Heat the cotechino in a saucepan of boiling water in the pouch in which it came (it's already cooked; you just need to heat it through, then remove it from its pouch). Keep the beef and chicken in the pot covered with the cooking liquid until you want to serve, then slice the beef, cotechino and chicken, removing the chicken skin. Either serve the meats in soup plates with broth spooned over (that's what I do) or take them to the table on a platter and bring the broth in a tureen. The important thing is not to have the meats out of the broth for longer than necessary, as they must stay moist.

Serve with the salsa verde and *mostarda di frutta* – a sweet and hot Italian condiment – on the side, and whole or halved carrots, quartered onions and celery sticks (simmered separately in stock). Something starchy – white beans or Umbrian lentils – is usually served as well.

mar i muntanya

This is Catalan, a 'surf 'n turf' dish, though their name for it translates, rather more poetically, as 'sea and mountain'. You should, ideally, use langoustines or Dublin Bay prawns. If you want to do that, buy about 24, leave them in their shells and add them three minutes before the end of cooking. I usually find that they're either very expensive or not very good quality (unless you are making this in Spain or in Ireland), so fall back on organically farmed king prawns.

You start, as you do in Catalan cooking, with a sofregit, *a mix of slow-cooked onions and tomatoes, and the dish is eventually thickened – and its flavour deepened – with a classic mixture of pounded bread, nuts, garlic and herbs called a* picada *(it's used elsewhere in the book, though not as a thickener).*

This isn't at all difficult or time-consuming to make, yet it makes its way into the Feast chapter because it is distinctive and deserves to be served with some fanfare… and some great wine.

SERVES 6–8

FOR THE CHICKEN
1½ tbsp olive oil
1 large chicken, jointed into 8,
    or 8 skin-on bone-in thighs
    and drumsticks
salt and pepper
2 large onions, finely chopped
5 really well-flavoured
    tomatoes, peeled, deseeded
    and chopped (see page 158)
500ml (18fl oz) dry white wine
    (or a mixture of white wine
    and fino sherry)
1½ tbsp anisette or pernod
400g (14oz) organic king
    prawns
¼ tbsp chopped flat-leaf
    parsley leaves

FOR THE PICADA
25g (scant 1oz) country bread,
    crusts removed
½ tbsp extra virgin olive oil
20 blanched almonds, toasted
3 garlic cloves, very finely
    chopped
leaves from 5 sprigs of parsley

Heat the regular oil in a broad, shallow casserole and brown the chicken joints until they are golden all over. Season as you are cooking them. Remove them as they're ready and set aside.

Pour off all but 1½ tbsp of the oil from the pan. You're now going to make the *sofregit*, the onion and tomato base. Heat the oil in the pan, add the onions and cook them slowly until they are soft and golden. It will take about 15 minutes and you might need to add a splash of water to keep the onions moist. Add the tomatoes, season and continue to cook, again slowly, until these are completely soft, 'jammy' and intensely flavoured. A lot of the liquid will evaporate during this time. It will probably take about another 15 minutes.

Add the wine and return the chicken, skin side up, with any of the juices that have run out of it. Bring to the boil, then reduce the heat to a very gentle simmer and cook, uncovered, for 40 minutes. Move the chicken round from time to time.

Make the *picada*. Fry the bread on both sides in the virgin oil over a high heat until crisp (it shouldn't soak up the oil or remain soggy). Put into a mortar with the almonds, garlic and parsley and pound to a rough paste, using a little of the chicken broth to moisten it. About 10 minutes before the end of cooking, stir in the *picada* and the anisette. Taste for seasoning.

Finally, two minutes before the end of cooking, add the prawns, gently stirring them in. They will turn pink and cook through. Taste again for seasoning and adjust if needed. I usually throw more parsley over the top before serving.

middle eastern rose-scented poussins with sour cherries and yogurt

It might seem odd to marinate anything in flower water, but it gives only a slight scent (and has strong spices to compete with). The roses bring a little romance (so it's good for a Valentine's dinner) but it's definitely not a girly dish, there are plenty of robust flavours here.

SERVES 4

FOR THE MARINADE

5 tbsp olive oil

3–4 tbsp rose water

2 tbsp pomegranate molasses

3 tsp ground cumin

3 tsp ground cinnamon

1 tsp cayenne pepper

4 garlic cloves, crushed

about 12 mint leaves, torn

2 tsp soft light brown sugar

salt and pepper

4 poussins

FOR THE DRESSING

4½ tbsp extra virgin olive oil
(fruity rather than grassy)

3 tbsp pomegranate molasses

2½ tsp runny honey, or to taste

3 tsp rose water

FOR THE YOGURT

40g (1½oz) dried sour cherries

½ cucumber

350g (12oz) Greek yogurt

1 garlic clove, crushed

2 tbsp extra virgin olive oil

10g (¼oz) walnuts, roughly
chopped

1 tbsp chopped mint leaves,
plus more to serve

unsprayed rose petals, to serve

Mix together the ingredients for the marinade and lay the poussins in a broad shallow dish. Pour the marinade on and turn the birds over in it. Cover loosely with cling film and put in the fridge. Marinate overnight if you have time, but just give it a couple of hours if that's all you have. Turn the birds over a few times while they are marinating.

To make the dressing, just whisk everything together.

Take the poussins out of the fridge 30 minutes before you want to cook them. Preheat the oven to 180°C/350°F/gas mark 4. Shake off the excess marinade, put in a roasting tin and roast the birds in the hot oven for 50 minutes.

Meanwhile, for the yogurt, soak the cherries in just-boiled water for 15 minutes so they plump up. Peel the cucumber, halve it, scoop out the seeds with a spoon and discard. Chop the cucumber flesh into small cubes and mix with the yogurt, garlic and half the extra virgin oil. Put into a flat bowl. Drain the sour cherries and sprinkle them across the top, then the walnuts too. Drizzle with the rest of the extra virgin oil and scatter with the mint.

Serve the poussins with the dressing spooned over them and the yogurt on the side. Scatter some more mint and the rose petals on top. Bitter leaves and bulgar wheat are good on the side.

royal chicken korma

Once I had made chicken korma myself, I was never able to order it from a takeaway again. This is based on a recipe from my great friend Roopa Gulati and it's simply stunning. Doubling the recipe – so it serves 12 generously – is easy, so you can really put on a feast. There are many variations on chicken korma, some include rose water and white poppy seeds, others coconut, but all are rich. I like this with a rice pilau with dried fruit. Wisps of edible gold or silver leaf added to the pilau is in keeping with the Moghul cooking style and will make your feast even more sumptuous. It's a joy to put this on the table.

SERVES 6

2 large onions, finely sliced,
   plus 2 onions, finely chopped
vegetable oil, to deep-fry
½ tsp saffron strands
25g (1oz) raw cashews, plus
   1 tbsp roasted, unsalted
   cashews, to serve
25g (1oz) blanched almonds
4 tbsp ghee, or clarified butter
½ tsp cloves
12 green cardamom pods,
   bruised (not broken)
5 black cardamom pods,
   bruised (not broken)
1 cinnamon stick, halved
800g (1lb 12oz) skinless
   boneless chicken thighs, cut
   into big chunks
4cm (1½in) root ginger, peeled
   and finely grated
4 garlic cloves, finely chopped
½ tsp red Kashmiri chilli
   powder
2 tsp toasted, ground coriander
   seeds (see page 66)
½ tsp ground white pepper
50g (1¾oz) plain yogurt
75ml (2½fl oz) double cream
good squeeze of lime juice
½ tsp garam masala
2 tbsp chopped coriander

Sprinkle the sliced onions liberally with salt, put in a sieve or colander and set aside for 30 minutes. Squeeze any excess liquid from the onions and pat them dry with kitchen paper.

Heat about 12.5cm (5in) of oil in a deep pan or a wok and deep-fry the salted onions in batches. When they turn golden, remove with a slotted spoon and drain on kitchen paper. Put the fried onions into a food processor with 75ml (2½fl oz) of hot water and process until you get a smooth paste. Set aside.

Soak the saffron strands in 3 tbsp of warm water and set aside for 30 minutes until the liquid turns a deep auburn (you really do have to leave it this long, don't rush or skip this step).

Prepare a nut paste: soak the raw cashews and the almonds in warm water for 15 minutes. Put the nuts into a food processor with 50ml (2fl oz) of the soaking liquid and purée.

Now you can start making the main curry base. Heat the ghee or clarified butter in a wok or heavy-based pan and cook the chopped onions for 10 minutes, until soft. Stir in the cloves, both types of cardamom and the cinnamon. Cook for a couple of minutes more. Now add the chicken thighs to the pan followed by the browned onion paste, ground nuts, ginger, garlic, chilli powder and crushed coriander seeds and white pepper. Season with salt. Increase the heat a little and continue frying everything together for another 10 minutes.

Pour 150ml (5fl oz) of hot water on to the chicken and simmer gently until the thighs are tender; this takes about 15 minutes.

Stir in the saffron liquid, yogurt and cream and heat through but don't boil. Taste for seasoning, then add a squeeze of lime juice and sprinkle on the garam masala, toasted cashews and chopped coriander. Serve with naan bread or rice and chutneys.

smoked paprika roast chicken, potato wedges and saffron allioli

A lovely, golden dish. It's only chicken and potatoes but the smoked paprika – the taste of Spain – and the saffron allioli takes it to a whole other level.

You can make the allioli the day before you want to serve it, cover and keep it in the fridge. A few caperberries – either on each plate or in a small bowl on the table – add another Hispanic touch.

SERVES 8

FOR THE CHICKEN AND POTATOES

6 tbsp olive oil, plus more for the potatoes

salt and pepper

4 tbsp smoked paprika

2.4kg (5lb 5oz) chicken

2kg (4lb 8oz) potatoes (don't peel them)

FOR THE ALLIOLI

2 garlic cloves, peeled

sea salt

2 egg yolks

300ml (½ pint) mild fruity olive oil

¼ tsp saffron strands

1 tbsp lemon juice, or to taste

ground white pepper

white wine vinegar, to taste (optional)

Preheat the oven to 180°C/350°F/gas mark 4. Mix the olive oil, salt and pepper and 3 tbsp of the paprika together. Paint or spoon this on to the chicken. Roast in the oven for 1 hour 50 minutes. It is cooked when the juices which run out between the leg and body are clear, with no trace of pink.

Meanwhile, make the allioli. Crush the garlic with a little sea salt in a large mortar and pestle, or a bowl. Stir in the egg yolks. Add the oil drop by drop, very slowly at first, beating with a wooden spoon or an electric hand mixer as you do so. Only add more oil once the previous lot has been incorporated and the mixture has thickened.

When you've added all the oil, heat the saffron in the lemon juice and leave to cool. Gradually add this to the allioli, taste and season with more salt, white pepper and any lemon (or vinegar) you think you need. It's better to taste as you go rather than sticking to specified amounts, as vinegars vary in strength. Cover and keep in the fridge.

Cut the potatoes into wedges, about 3.5cm (1½in) at their widest, put them in a roasting tin, add a couple of tbsp of oil and sprinkle with salt and pepper and the remaining smoked paprika. Turn everything over with your hands. Put them in the oven to cook in the final 20 minutes of the chicken's cooking time. (That way they can cook while the chicken is resting.) Give them a shake halfway to move them around a bit.

When the chicken is cooked, cover it with foil. Leave it to rest for 15 minutes while the wedges finish cooking, before serving with the potatoes and the allioli. This dish can take the grand treatment: put the bird on a heated platter and pile the wedges around it. Serve with the allioli and a green salad, or sautéed spinach with pine nuts and raisins.

roast chicken with truffles

Before you conclude that I've gone quite mad with the cash, consider this: this is a lovely dish, special, a real treat, something you can enjoy with your partner or a few good friends. In my life, I've made it on only a handful of occasions (though never before now with fresh truffles) and I've never regretted it. Depending on how flush you are, this dish can be incredibly expensive to make or – at the other end of the scale – cheaper than buying four takeaway pizzas. In descending order of expense you can use fresh black truffles (summer are cheaper than winter truffles), truffles that are frozen or in jars in their own juice, or sliced truffles preserved in oil. The price of fresh truffles varies. The cheapest form – sliced black summer truffles in oil – costs about £7.50 for 30g/1oz (about the amount you need for this dish). You get what you pay for but even the sliced and preserved truffles, in my opinion, are gorgeous. Since you are cooking with truffles it makes sense to get the best bird you can afford. You could buy the best your local butcher provides, or a Label Anglais, or go all out and buy a Bresse chicken (you can read more about 'high end' chickens in the introduction). All forms of truffles – and truffle butter – can be found online.

SERVES 4

sea salt flakes ·
1.5kg (3lb 5oz) chicken
30g (1oz) black truffle, sliced or shaved
25g (scant 1oz) unsalted butter
300ml (½ pint) good home-made chicken stock
30g (1oz) truffle butter

Start 24 hours before you want to cook the dish: salt the bird, then put it in the fridge. Bring the chicken to room temperature. Preheat the oven to 210°C/410°F/gas mark 6½.

Carefully loosen the skin of the breast and legs of the bird (see page 101). Put slices of truffle – keeping a few back to add to the sauce – under the skin. Put into an ovenproof dish (a copper or cast-iron one is good) of a size in which the bird will sit snugly. Rub the regular butter all over the breast and legs. Put into the hot oven – the legs should be toward the back of the oven – and cook for 50 minutes (check for doneness by looking at the juices that run out between the leg and the body of the bird, they should have no trace of pink). Transfer the chicken to a warmed platter, put a foil tent over it to keep it warm and let it rest.

Pour off most of the fat (it has such a good flavour I keep it for frying potatoes) and set the dish on the hob. Deglaze with a bit of the stock (obviously not so much that the pan is overflowing) and stir and scrape up the dried-on bits with a wooden spoon. Transfer this to a saucepan, add the rest of the stock and boil until you have about 150ml (5fl oz). Add the truffle butter a bit at a time, whisking with a small whisk (the sauce will turn glossy) then stir in the reserved truffle slices. Joint and serve at the table, offering the sauce in small warmed jug.

I love this with sautéed potatoes and some watercress.

jewish chicken with tzimmes

I first had this for lunch at the home of a Jewish friend who knew I would love the sweet-savoury flavours (at first, I thought it was a Moroccan dish). The word tzimmes *means 'to make a fuss over somebody or something' so I suppose that's why it's such a mixture. It's a dish of root vegetables and fresh and dried fruit that is cooked around the chicken – and is very sweet – but you can tone it down by adding less dried fruit and replacing some of the sweeter vegetables (the carrots and sweet potatoes) with ordinary potatoes, if you want. (Carrots are very important at Jewish New Year though, as they are symbolic of the good deeds you hope to do in the coming year, so if you're making it for Rosh Hashanah it's best not to tamper with the carrots!)*

SERVES 8

2kg (4lb 8oz) chicken
1 tbsp extra virgin olive oil
salt and pepper
500g (1lb 2oz) carrots, long slim ones if possible
550g (1lb 4oz) sweet potatoes, peeled and sliced
3 tart apples, halved, cored and cut into wedges
12 prunes
finely grated zest and juice of 1 orange
250ml (9fl oz) chicken stock
250ml (9fl oz) red or white wine
2cm (¾in) root ginger, peeled and grated
½ tsp ground cinnamon
2 tbsp soft light brown sugar, or to taste
juice of ⅓ lemon
½ tbsp finely chopped flat-leaf parsley leaves (optional)

Preheat the oven to 180°C/350°F/gas mark 4. Put the chicken into a roasting tin, big enough for the vegetables and fruit to fit around it. Rub with the olive oil and season with salt and pepper.

Peel the carrots if they need it, or wash thoroughly. Leave whole if they are slim, cut in half lengthways if they aren't. Put the carrots, sweet potatoes, apples and prunes round the chicken (tuck the prunes underneath as they will burn if exposed). Heat the orange zest and juice with the stock, wine, ginger and cinnamon. Pour over the vegetables. Sprinkle on the sugar and season.

Put into the hot oven and cook for 1 hour 25 minutes, basting the chicken every so often with the juices. If, at the end of cooking time, you still have quite a lot of liquid, you can remove the chicken, veg and fruit to a heated platter and reduce the liquid by boiling. This is supposed to be a sweet dish, but make sure the juices don't become off-puttingly sweet when you boil them. Squeeze the lemon juice over the vegetables and sprinkle with the parsley.

My friend Helen serves this for Rosh Hashanah with potatoes roasted in chicken fat.

chicken fatteh

A feast with lots of elements, textures and temperatures. Layer the components judiciously, each needs wise seasoning. And be generous with the herbs, to make it sing. Finish with pomegranate seeds and pistachios.

SERVES 8–10

FOR THE TOMATO SAUCE
4 tbsp olive oil
1 onion, very finely chopped
4 garlic cloves, crushed
¼ tsp ground cinnamon
2 x 400g cans of tomatoes
½ tsp soft light brown sugar

FOR THE CHICKEN
1.8kg (4lb) chicken
3 tbsp olive oil
½ tsp ground cumin
¼ tsp ground cinnamon
¼ tsp ground cloves

FOR THE RICE
300g (10½oz) basmati rice
25g (scant 1oz) unsalted butter
1 tbsp olive oil
1 onion, finely sliced
¼ tsp ground cinnamon
½ tsp ground cumin
500ml (18fl oz) chicken stock

FOR THE REST
2 pitta breads
25g (1oz) butter, melted
8 tbsp olive oil
4 aubergines, in 3cm/1¼in cubes
3 tsp ground cumin
1 tsp dried chilli flakes
squeezes of lemon juice
1 garlic clove, crushed
500g (1lb 2oz) Greek yogurt
large handfuls of chopped
    parsley and coriander leaves
50g (1¾oz) pine nuts, toasted

Preheat the oven to 180°C/350°F/gas mark 4. For the sauce, heat the oil and cook the onion until soft and pale gold. Add the garlic and cinnamon and cook for two minutes. Add the tomatoes, seasoning, sugar and 100ml (3½fl oz) of water. Simmer, uncovered, for 30 minutes. Heat the pittas in the oven for a couple of minutes, then split and brush with melted butter. Cut in triangles and bake for 10 minutes, until crisp.

Put the chicken in a roasting tin and rub the oil over it, season and massage with the spices. Roast for 1 hour 15 minutes, basting. It is ready when the juices between the leg and body run clear with no trace of pink. Transfer to a dish to rest for 15 minutes, covered with foil. Put the tin over a medium heat, add 200ml (7fl oz) of water and bring to a simmer, scraping up any bits. Cook until you have about 100ml (3½fl oz) of liquid left.

Wash the rice well. Heat the butter and oil in a saucepan and fry the onion for 12 minutes, until golden, stirring now and then. Add the spices and cook for two minutes. Set aside. When the chicken is cooler, tear the meat into pieces. Keep warm.

Heat 4 tbsp of olive oil over a medium-high heat, add half the aubergines and fry until soft and golden. Add half the spices, season well and squeeze on lemon juice. Keep warm. Repeat.

About 30 minutes before eating, add the rice to the onions. Add the stock and boil hard until the surface of the rice looks pitted. Reduce the heat to its lowest, cover and cook for 17 minutes. Don't stir it but do check to make sure it isn't sticking.

Now layer the components in a large dish. Everything should be hot apart from the bread and yogurt, so reheat the sauce. Stir the garlic into the yogurt. Squeeze lemon juice on the layers as you go and sprinkle most of the herbs on too. Start with pitta, then rice, then chicken – seasoned and mixed with 5 tbsp of its gravy – then aubergine, tomato sauce and yogurt. Scatter with more herbs, the pine nuts, pomegranate seeds and pistachios with a drizzle more yogurt (serve the rest on the side).

summer and smoke *griddled and barbecued*

chicken piri piri

Whenever I go to Portugal my first pit stop is the same: a chicken piri piri restaurant that is little more than a shack (there are no real walls, just bits of matting hung on a frame) at the side of a dusty road. The place is full of Portuguese families noisily shouting for more piri piri sauce. Nothing else is served. Just frango piri piri, *salad and chips or bread. The chicken is cooked on huge braziers and it's difficult to replicate the special smokiness when you cook it at home, but you can almost get it. The Portuguese piri piri I've eaten always has a great red colour and is slightly sweet. I've tried to replicate this here by adding roast pepper.*

It's hard to be prescriptive about cooking times as it depends on your grill (and some domestic grills are very poor), so these instructions are guidelines only. If you prefer to roast your joints, put them on a rack set in a roasting tin and cook for 40 minutes in an oven preheated to 220°C/425°F/gas mark 7.

In Portugal, whole small chickens or poussins – spatchcocked – are cooked this way, so use those if you prefer (get your butcher to do the spatchcocking). There is enough piri piri here for four poussins. Roast them just as you would joints.

SERVES 6

1 small red pepper
50ml (2fl oz) olive oil
4 red chillies
4 garlic cloves, crushed
2 tsp dried oregano, or
   chopped fresh oregano
   leaves
½ tsp chilli flakes
2 tbsp red wine vinegar
juice of 2 lemons
½ tsp caster sugar
1 tsp sea salt flakes
6 skin-on bone-in chicken
   legs (drumsticks and thighs
   attached)

Preheat the oven to 190°C/375°F/gas mark 5. Halve and deseed the pepper, brush with a little of the oil, put into a small tin and roast until its flesh is soft (about 25 minutes). Peel the skin off if it comes off easily; leave it if it doesn't. Chop roughly, then crush in a mortar and pestle. Set aside.

Remove the stems from the chillies and deseed them. Chop finely, then put into an empty mortar with the garlic, oregano and chilli flakes. Pound to a rough paste, then add the vinegar, lemon juice, sugar, salt, remaining oil and red pepper. Put the chicken into a broad, shallow dish and pour on most of the marinade. Turn to coat, cover with cling film and put in the fridge for about four hours (overnight is even better), turning a couple of times. Bring to room temperature before cooking.

Heat your grill and arrange the chicken on the grill pan, skin side up. Place the grill pan 10cm (4in) from the heat and grill for 12 minutes on each side, reducing the heat halfway through. Baste every so often with the juices or a little more marinade.

Move the chicken another 10cm (4in) from the heat and grill for another six or seven minutes on each side. The chicken should be cooked through (make sure the juices are clear and there is no trace of pink), sizzling and dark red.

Serve immediately with a lettuce, cucumber and tomato salad and fried potatoes or coarse country bread.

chicken with griddled leeks, roast peppers and salbitxada

Salbitxada is a Catalan sauce. It most often ends up fairly finely ground – like a purée, or pesto – but I like to find chunks of tomato in it, it's much fresher. You can, if you prefer, make it in the food processor, but a mortar and pestle gives a good chunky result.

The chicken doesn't have to be breasts, this is just as good with a roast chicken (in fact it makes a fabulous big feast when served with loads of roast peppers and griddled leeks). Don't feel restricted to leeks and peppers either; you can serve griddled artichoke hearts or asparagus as well. Want to make it simpler? Just go with the chicken, the sauce, one vegetable and sprigs of watercress.

SERVES 6

FOR THE CHICKEN

6 skinless boneless chicken
  breasts
3 tbsp extra virgin olive oil
finely grated zest and juice of
  1 unwaxed lemon
3 red peppers
olive oil
salt and pepper
18–24 baby leeks, trimmed
pea shoots, to serve

FOR THE SALBITXADA

250g (9oz) tomatoes
2 garlic cloves, very finely
  chopped
sea salt flakes
3 tbsp blanched almonds,
  lightly toasted
1 red chilli, halved, deseeded
  and chopped
4 tbsp finely chopped flat-leaf
  parsley leaves
½ tbsp sherry vinegar, or
  to taste
6 tbsp extra virgin olive oil
  (ideally Spanish), or to taste

Put the chicken between two sheets of greaseproof paper and bash with a rolling pin (a couple of bashes is enough). Put in a dish with the virgin oil, lemon zest and juice. Cover and leave for 30 minutes (more if you have time) in the fridge. Preheat the oven to 190°C/375°F/gas mark 5. Put the peppers in a roasting tin, drizzle with regular oil and season. Cook them in the oven for 40 minutes, until soft and scorched in places.

Meanwhile, make the sauce. Drop the tomatoes into boiling water for 20 seconds or so, then run cold water over them and peel off the skins (I sometimes can't be bothered). Halve the tomatoes, scoop out the seeds and core and chop the flesh.

Put the garlic and salt into a mortar and pound to a paste. Add the almonds and chilli and pound these. Now add the parsley and tomatoes and pound, but mix with a fork too, so the ingredients are combined but don't form a purée. Stir in the vinegar, virgin oil and pepper. Taste to check if you need more oil or vinegar. It should be assertive but balanced.

Cut the peppers into slices, lengthways. I don't remove the skin – I like the taste – but if it comes off naturally, discard it. Try to time things so the leeks and chicken are ready at the same time. Brush the leeks with regular oil and season. Heat a griddle pan and cook the leeks for about five minutes, turning, until nicely coloured. Reduce the heat and cook until tender.

Heat a frying or griddle pan, season the chicken and cook for about four minutes on each side. It should be cooked through. Serve on a platter with the leeks, peppers and pea shoots, with some of the sauce spooned over the top and the rest on the side.

chicken shish with toum

Chicken kebabs are ubiquitous all over the Middle East and are one of the easiest things to make for a barbecue. I prefer chicken thighs (it's much juicier meat) but they are always more ragged; you can cut breast fillets into much neater chunks. Do whichever you prefer. After years of using wooden skewers I now always use metal ones, as they help the meat cook by conducting heat into the centre of the chicken pieces. (You can also use the marinade on whole skinless boneless thighs and just griddle them, if you don't want to make kebabs.)

Toum is Lebanese garlic purée – quite like a Catalan allioli – and is for serious garlic lovers. The oil has to be added carefully and gradually – just as if you were making mayonnaise – until you have a thick emulsion. It will end up pale, almost snowy looking. It makes a wonderful paste to spread on warm flatbread; just put your skewered chicken on top. This quantity makes more than you need for the recipe but it's very hard to make it in a food processor in smaller amounts.

SERVES 6 8

FOR THE CHICKEN

1kg (2lb 4oz) skinless boneless chicken thighs or breasts
2 tbsp Aleppo pepper
1 tbsp ground coriander
1¼ tbsp ground cumin
juice of 2 lemons
8 garlic cloves, grated
6 tbsp olive oil
Greek yogurt, to serve

FOR THE TOUM

4 bulbs of garlic, cloves separated and peeled
350ml (12fl oz) mixed groundnut and olive oils
½ tsp sea salt flakes, or more to taste
juice of 1½ lemons, or more to taste
100ml (3½fl oz) iced water

Cut the chicken into chunks, about 4 x 2.5cm (1¾ x 1in). Put these in a bowl and add the rest of the ingredients. Cover and marinate in the fridge for four hours (or longer, if you can). Bring to room temperature before cooking.

For the toum, halve each garlic clove and remove any green shoots inside. Put in a food processor and blitz to a purée, stopping the machine to push the garlic down the sides. You're aiming to end up with a smooth purée. Now start adding the oil a tiny drizzle at a time, with the motor running, as if you were making mayonnaise, but taking even more care. Stop every so often and stir the mixture. Add the salt and, still with the motor running, add the lemon juice and iced water. Taste. You may want more salt or lemon juice. Scrape into a bowl.

Thread the cubes of chicken on to skewers (if you are using thighs make sure you tuck in any extraneous bits). You can cook them on either a griddle pan or the barbecue. If you're using the barbecue, put them on to the rack when the flames have died down but the embers are still hot, placing them round the edge. It should take about eight minutes to cook them through; you need to turn them as they cook. If you're doing them on the griddle, heat it until it's very hot, lay the kebabs on it and cook, turning every so often and adjusting the heat, until the chicken is cooked through.

Serve with warm flatbread, a salad of leaves, cucumbers and tomatoes, Greek yogurt and the toum.

barbecued poussins with za'atar and roast pumpkin houmous

You can buy za'atar – a Middle Eastern spice blend – but it's easy to make your own (and cheap, too). Making it yourself also means you can vary it. This is a very basic za'atar, others are more complicated, but thyme, sumac and sesame seeds are essential. It makes more than you need, but keep it in an airtight container and sprinkle it on warm flatbread, or use it to marinate lamb kebabs. Pumpkin houmous isn't authentic but it gives chickpea houmous a run for its money. I vary the ingredients, sometimes adding ground cumin or dried chilli (add those when you roast the pumpkin or when you purée it). What is really important is seasoning and adding the right amount of lemon juice, so use your taste buds.

SERVES 4

FOR THE ZA'ATAR

small bunch of thyme,
    (enough to give about 4 tbsp
    of thyme leaves)
2 tsp ground sumac
½ tbsp dried wild oregano
1 tbsp sesame seeds, toasted
1 tsp sea salt flakes

FOR THE POUSSINS

juice of 1 lemon, plus lemon
    wedges to serve
4 garlic cloves, crushed
6 tbsp olive oil
salt and pepper
4 poussins, spatchcocked

FOR THE HOUMOUS

800g (1lb 12oz) pumpkin or
    butternut squash
2 tbsp olive oil
135g (4¾oz) cooked chickpeas
2 garlic cloves, finely chopped
2½ tbsp tahini
juice of 1 lemon
50ml (2fl oz) extra virgin
    olive oil

First of all make the za'atar. Preheat the oven to 150°C/300°F/gas mark 2. Strip the leaves from the thyme. Put them in a small roasting tin and bake in the oven for about 10 minutes. Put the dried leaves into a mortar and pound lightly. Add the remaining ingredients. Pound a little more, but not so much that you grind the sesame seeds, just to release the aromas.

Mix 4 tbsp of the za'atar with the lemon juice, garlic, olive oil and pepper. Trim any raggedy bits of skin from the poussins. Put them in a dish and cover them in the marinade. Cover with cling film and put in the fridge for four hours or overnight. Bring to room temperature before cooking.

Preheat the oven to 200°C/400°F/gas mark 6. Cut the pumpkin into chunks then remove the seeds and peel. Put into a roasting tin, drizzle with the regular oil, season and roast for about 25 minutes, until completely tender.

Prepare a barbecue to the stage where the coals are hot but no longer flaming. Lift the poussins out of the marinade and put on to the barbecue. Cook for 10 minutes, then turn and cook for another 10 minutes. Check to see if they are done and return the poussins if they need more cooking, changing their position on the barbecue. It usually takes 25 minutes in all.

Quickly purée the pumpkin with the other ingredients for the houmous. Sprinkle the poussins with more za'atar and serve with the houmous and some Greek yogurt. You don't need any starch, as the houmous provides that, but a green salad, tomato salad, or roast tomatoes are lovely on the side. Provide lemon wedges as well, to squeeze on the poussins.

ginger beer can chicken

This is honestly a basic guide from which you can spin off in all sorts of directions. First of all you can use different beers (I have even used honey porter in the past), or a mixture of beers. Make it spicier, use different herbs, add mustard, citrus juice, whatever. Play around. The only thing that's important is the beer and the technique of cooking. A few have complained that the method doesn't actually work, that you don't need to put the open beer can inside the bird, but part of the fun – in my house anyway – is in getting the bird on and off the barbecue with the can in it. And it's always damned delicious, moist and smoky.

You do need tomato sauce, not ketchup. Use regular beer if you prefer, but my kids love this version.

SERVES 6

1.8kg (4lb) chicken

FOR THE TOMATO SAUCE
1 tbsp olive oil
1 onion, finely chopped
2 garlic cloves, finely chopped
400g can of tomatoes
salt and pepper
¼ tsp soft light brown sugar

FOR THE MARINADE
400ml (14fl oz) ginger beer,
    plus 300ml can of
    ginger beer
125ml (4fl oz) good-quality
    tomato sauce, preferably
    home-made (see above)
40g (1½oz) root ginger, peeled
    and grated
6 garlic cloves, grated
4 red chillies, stalks removed,
    finely chopped (I leave the
    seeds in)
¾ tbsp smoked paprika
leaves from 8 sprigs of thyme
3 tbsp soft dark brown sugar

To make the tomato sauce, heat the olive oil in a saucepan and gently sauté the onion until soft but not coloured. Add the garlic and cook for another minute. Stir in the tomatoes, 125ml (4fl oz) of water, the seasoning and sugar. Bring to the boil, then reduce the heat to a simmer and cook for 30 minutes, making sure it doesn't become too dry. Leave to cool, then purée.

Mix 100ml of the beer in a large bowl, big enough to contain the chicken, with all the other marinade ingredients. Put the chicken in the bowl, too, and rub the marinade all over it inside and out. Cover loosely with foil or cling film and put in the fridge for eight hours. Then remove from the fridge and pour over the remaining 300ml (½ pint) of ginger beer plus 100ml of the canned stuff (keep the rest in the can). Cover, return to the fridge and marinate for 24 hours, turning every so often.

Prepare a lidded barbecue to the stage where the coals are hot but no longer flaming. Shake the marinade off the chicken and pat dry with kitchen paper. Season. Place the chicken on the opened ginger beer can so the can is in the cavity. Place the can and chicken on to a rack off the barbecue, then put the rack on to the barbecue so that the base of the can is on the rack and the chicken is sitting upright. Be careful. It's a little tricky to balance everything as you put the rack down on to the barbecue (because it's hot) but persevere and get help!

Close the lid and cook for 40–45 minutes, then pierce the chicken between the leg and the body: the juices should have no trace of pink. If it's not finished, continue to cook. Carefully take the chicken off the can, carve and serve.

pomegranate and honey-glazed chicken skewers

These look very pretty. They make good picnic food, too. If I'm taking them on a picnic I usually make a little fresh marinade (don't use the marinade in which the chicken has already been steeping; you must make fresh stuff) and brush the chicken skewers with it before packing them. It helps keep them moist. Don't forget that wooden skewers need to be soaked in water in advance for about 30 minutes; this stops them burning on the griddle.

SERVES 4

FOR THE MARINADE

2½ tbsp pomegranate molasses
150ml (5fl oz) olive oil, plus a little more to fry (optional)
1½ tbsp runny honey
2 garlic cloves, crushed
3 tsp cayenne pepper
½ tbsp ground coriander
1 tbsp ground cumin
salt and pepper

FOR THE CHICKEN

8 skinless boneless chicken thighs
½ red onion, cut wafer-thin (use a mandoline if you have one)
bunch of coriander
15g (½oz) roughly chopped pistachios
3 tbsp extra virgin olive oil
1 tbsp lemon juice
pomegranate seeds, to serve (optional)

Mix everything for the marinade together in a shallow dish. Cut the chicken into chunks, about 2cm (¾in) square. Put the chicken in the marinade, turning to coat, cover with cling film and leave in the fridge overnight. Bring to room temperature before cooking. Thread the chicken pieces on to skewers and season with salt and pepper.

Heat a griddle pan and cook the skewers over a medium heat, turning them to cook on all sides. If you don't have a griddle pan, heat a little oil in a large frying pan and cook them in that. Either way, it takes about 10 minutes. Be careful not to burn the outside of the chicken before the inside is cooked (this is easily done because of the honey in the marinade). Adjust your heat accordingly.

Toss the onion, coriander and pistachios lightly with the virgin oil and lemon. Season. Put the salad on a big platter. Put the hot skewers on the platter, too and scatter with pomegranate seeds (if using). A bowl of Greek yogurt, into which you have stirred some chopped mint leaves and crushed garlic, is lovely with this. Flatbread or bulgar wheat make good starchy side dishes.

indian-spiced chicken with coriander chutney

Good for a midweek supper, or equally enjoyable cooked on the barbecue in summer. The chicken becomes lovely and smoky. Make sure you leave it to marinate properly, it really makes a difference. A tomato marinade might seem extravagant, so cook it when they are cheap and abundant, or when you have a glut of tomatoes that are past their best (a bit soft).

SERVES 4

FOR THE CHICKEN

250g (9oz) tomatoes, roughly
   chopped
1 tsp tomato purée
1½ tsp cumin seeds, toasted
   and ground (see page 66)
1½ tsp coriander seeds, toasted
   and ground (see page 66)
4 garlic cloves, chopped
3cm (1¼in) root ginger, peeled
   and chopped
salt and pepper
½ green chilli, deseeded and
   chopped
4 skinless boneless chicken
   breasts or thighs
2 tbsp rapeseed oil (or any
   other oil you prefer)

FOR THE CHUTNEY

50g (1¾oz) coriander leaves
   and stalks, separated
1 green chilli, halved, deseeded
   and chopped
juice of 2 limes, plus more
   if needed
2 garlic cloves, chopped
2cm (¾in) root ginger, peeled
   and chopped
1 tsp cumin seeds, toasted
   (see page 66)
1 tsp caster sugar

Put everything for the chicken – except the chicken itself and the oil – into a food processor with the coriander stalks (from the chutney ingredients list). Whizz to a rough purée.

If the chicken breasts are very thick, cut them in half horizontally. Whether you're using breasts or thighs, pierce them all over with the point of a sharp knife. Put the chicken into a dish and pour the puréed tomato mixture all over them. Turn them over in the marinade, cover with cling film and put in the fridge for two hours (or overnight). Turn the chicken pieces over every so often. Bring to room temperature before cooking.

To make the chutney, put the coriander leaves into a food processor with all the other ingredients and whizz. Taste. You might need more lime juice. Scrape into a bowl.

Heat a griddle until it's very hot. Lift the chicken out of its marinade and brush the pieces on each side with the oil. Cook on a high heat for about three minutes, turning once (and moving the chicken round the griddle so that no pieces are cooking in the less-hot patches). Season. Reduce the heat and cook for about two minutes, or until the chicken is cooked through (but not overcooked, it should still be moist). Thighs will take longer than breasts.

Serve the chicken with the coriander chutney, a bowl of cucumber raita and some rice. (I must say I also love a mango and watercress salad with it, but I always love a mango and watercress salad…)

thyme-griddled chicken with smoky chilli butter

Easy – it's just griddled chicken with a flavoured butter – but mouth-wateringly good. Perfect for a summer supper, or a cool early autumn evening.

SERVES 8

FOR THE BUTTER
250g (9oz) unsalted butter, at room temperature
3 garlic cloves, finely chopped
2 red chillies, halved, deseeded and finely chopped
3 tsp smoked paprika
leaves from 4 sprigs of thyme, plus more sprigs to serve
juice of ½ lemon

FOR THE CHICKEN
8–16 skinless boneless chicken thighs
olive oil
about 1 tbsp cayenne pepper
salt and pepper

To make the butter, just mash all the ingredients together and refrigerate. When the butter has firmed up, put it on to a piece of greaseproof paper and roll it into a neat sausage shape. Wrap in the paper and chill.

Hammer the chicken thighs so that they are flattened (use a meat mallet or a rolling pin). Brush with oil and season with cayenne pepper, salt and pepper.

Heat a griddle pan and cook the chicken on both sides, initially on a high heat to get a good colour. Do not turn the chicken thighs until they will lift easily from the pan, or you will tear the flesh. Reduce the heat under the griddle to cook right through (about eight minutes).

Serve the chicken with a round of the flavoured butter on top; it will start to melt as soon as it hits the hot flesh. Scatter with sprigs of thyme.

buttermilk chicken with chipotle slaw

Buttermilk does amazing things to chicken, tenderizing and flavouring the flesh right to the bone. It's a favourite treatment among American cooks and has become one of mine (I had previously only used buttermilk for making cakes and soda bread). The slaw is from the boys at Pitt Cue, the London gaff (I'm not sure it can really be called a restaurant as most people leave with food splashed down their fronts) that has put barbecue (and all things connected to it) firmly on the hipster map. Richard Turner, chef in them there parts, has allowed me to use it (I've changed it only slightly). He's a doll who, despite being a worshipper of all things porcine, makes bloody good salads.

You can cook this in the oven as well as on the barbecue, so I've given instructions for both.

SERVES 6–8

FOR THE CHICKEN
500ml (18fl oz) buttermilk
6 garlic cloves, crushed
½ tbsp cayenne pepper
salt and pepper
12 skin-on bone-in chicken
    thighs

FOR THE SLAW
½ white cabbage, cored and
    shredded
¼ red cabbage, cored and
    shredded
finely grated zest of 1 lime,
    plus juice of 2, or more
    to taste
1 garlic clove, grated
150g (5½oz) mayonnaise
25g (scant 1oz) canned
    chipotles in adobo, puréed,
    or 2 tbsp chipotle paste, or
    to taste
2 big tbsp soured cream
leaves from 1 bunch of
    coriander, chopped
a little extra virgin olive oil,
    if needed

Mix together the buttermilk, garlic and cayenne with plenty of salt and pepper. Using a small sharp knife, cut slits in the fleshy bits of the chicken thighs without piercing the skin. Put it in a dish and pour over the marinade. Turn the pieces, cover and refrigerate for 24 hours, turning every so often. Bring to room temperature before cooking.

To cook on the barbecue: prepare the barbecue and get it to the stage where the coals are hot but no longer flaming. Shake off the excess marinade then gently wipe the chicken with kitchen paper so that no buttermilk will drip on to the coals (or it creates flames that burn the chicken). Set on the rack, cover with a lid and cook for 40–45 minutes, turning halfway. Check for doneness: the juice that runs when you pierce the flesh near the bone should be clear with no trace of pink.

Or preheat the oven to 190°C/375°F/gas mark 5. Gently shake off the excess marinade (but don't wipe the chicken). Put the joints into a roasting tin. Roast for 40 minutes, or until cooked through. Cover with foil if the surface is getting too dark.

Meanwhile, make the slaw. Put both cabbages into a bowl and toss in the lime zest and juice, the garlic and salt and pepper.

Mix the mayonnaise with the chipotles. Add the soured cream and carefully stir this into the cabbage with the coriander. You might want to adjust now according to both taste and texture. If the mixture is too thick I sometimes add 1–2 tbsp of extra virgin olive oil. Flavour wise you might want a little more chipotle or lime juice.

Serve the chicken thighs on a platter with the slaw on the side.

a nice bit of thigh

My dad used to stand by the roast chicken, carving knife poised, and ask who wanted breast and who wanted thigh. The more he was asked for breast, the more he would sigh. For him, chicken breast is relatively bland and can easily become dry, while the thigh – succulent, with meat you want to suck from the bones and a good covering of crispy skin to boot – is glorious. Graduating to thigh meat was, in my family, a sign that you had grown up.

Chicken thighs loom larger in my repertoire of no-hassle dishes than any other ingredient. With a jointed chicken the various pieces cook at different rates, but a panful of chicken thighs will all be ready together and there's no fighting over who gets what. Griddled or fried, skinless boneless thighs have much more flavour than chicken breasts and can be topped with flavoured butters or relishes or drizzled with pesto. Or the pan can be deglazed with a good slug of booze to make a simple sauté. Thighs are the best cut for kebabs, too: fierce griddling or barbecuing produces a deliciously caramelized exterior with a juicy interior.

The way I most often cook thighs is to roast them, in one of two ways, as you'll notice in the recipes in this book. The first is to mix the chicken with ingredients that flavour the dish as it cooks: blanched fennel and chunks of chorizo; branches of rosemary; wrinkly black olives and wedges of orange. Everything is simply moistened with olive oil, seasoned and bunged in the oven. One-dish cooking at its very best. Be sure, though, that the various components cook at the same pace, or are added to the dish at the right stage. You can also do this kind of roasting – where the chicken is simply moistened – with thighs that have been marinated. The chicken stays moist but ends up with lovely burnished, savoury skin. Marinate thighs in honey and mustard, maple syrup with bourbon or chilli, or pomegranate molasses with garlic, olive oil and cumin. You'll end up with very different dishes despite having cooked the thighs in exactly the same way.

My other method of roasting is akin to pot-roasting, in fact I've heard it referred to as 'braise roasting'. With this I cook thighs with stock (or a mixture of stock and booze) that lies around the chicken, leaving the skin-covered tops (scattered with flakes of sea salt) sticking out so they can brown and crisp. The cooking vessel needs to be broad and shallow and should remain uncovered so the liquid evaporates as it cooks. What you end up with is a casserole-like dish without the hassle of browning the meat or reducing the cooking liquid. Chicken with sliced potatoes, onions, carrots and thyme, or with green olives, saffron-infused stock and preserved lemons, cooks to succulent perfection this way. It's one of the easiest approaches to the evening meal I know. The oven makes all the effort. But the reason it works so well is the moist succulence of the bit of the chicken I wouldn't even eat until I was 14: the thighs.

coriander-seared chicken with hot-and-cold cucumber relish

I cannot resist the combination of cold ingredients with hot, both in temperature and in spiciness. In my previous book, A Change of Appetite, *there was a dish of chilled cucumber with chilli and pickled ginger that everyone loved, so I'm revisiting the idea. The salad here is adapted from a recipe in* Hot, Sour, Salty, Sweet *by Jeffrey Alford and Naomi Duguid; they came across the dish in Yunnan. You can serve a chilli sauce on the side as well, but there is something pure and simple about just having chicken and cucumber.*

SERVES 4

FOR THE CHICKEN

6 garlic cloves, finely chopped
2 tsp black peppercorns
about 6 tbsp coarsely chopped
    coriander leaves
1 tbsp Thai fish sauce
juice of 1½ limes
8 skinless boneless chicken
    thighs
1½ tbsp groundnut oil

FOR THE CUCUMBER

1 large cucumber
3 tbsp rice vinegar
2 tbsp caster sugar
3 tbsp groundnut oil
1 red chilli, halved, deseeded
    and finely sliced
1 green chilli, halved, deseeded
    and finely sliced
4 small, very hot dried chillies,
    crumbled
8 Sichuan peppercorns
small handful of coriander
    leaves
¼ tsp salt

Start with the chicken. Put the garlic and peppercorns into a mortar and crush them, then add the coriander and continue until you have a rough paste. Add the fish sauce and lime juice. Put the chicken thighs in a dish and pour over the paste. Turn the chicken over with your hands, to coat. Cover loosely with cling film and put in the fridge for about four hours. Bring to room temperature before cooking.

Now for the cucumber. Peel it and halve lengthways. Cut into four lengths and scoop out the seeds using a teaspoon (discard them). Bash the cucumber with a rolling pin, then break it into pieces with your hands. This might seem odd, but it helps the flesh to absorb other flavours. Put the rice vinegar and sugar into a bowl and stir to dissolve the sugar. Add the cucumber and put in the coldest bit of the fridge (you can even stick it in the freezer for the time it takes you to griddle the chicken).

Heat the griddle pan, brush some oil over the chicken pieces and throw them on the griddle. Cook over a high heat to get a good colour on both sides, then reduce the heat until cooked right through (it will take seven or eight minutes in all, though thighs vary greatly in size, even when from the same packet; very annoying). The coriander and garlic from the marinade that sticks to the chicken will turn dark and charred, but it's delicious so don't panic about that (but don't burn the garlic!).

Heat the oil for the cucumber in a frying pan or wok until it is really hot and stir-fry the fresh chillies, dried chillies and peppercorns for about 30 seconds. Pour this over the cucumber, sprinkle on the coriander and salt and serve with the chicken. Brown rice is good on the side, if you want something starchy.

negima yakitori

This is a popular Japanese yakitori dish. There it is made with a vegetable called negi, *a kind of Japanese long onion. Here, fat spring onions are the things to use. Togarashi is a hot, citrussy Japanese spice blend. Waitrose now sell an own-label version, or you can easily get it online.*

If you're using wooden skewers, soak them in water for 30 minutes so that they don't burn.

SERVES 4–6

FOR THE YAKITORI SAUCE

250ml (9fl oz) soy sauce
125ml (4fl oz) sake or dry sherry
125ml (4fl oz) mirin
3 tbsp soft light brown sugar
4 garlic cloves, crushed
3cm (1¼in) root ginger, peeled and grated

FOR THE SKEWERS

900g (2lb) skinless boneless chicken thighs
16 spring onions
salt and pepper
flavourless vegetable oil (optional)
togarashi and sesame seeds, to sprinkle

Put all the ingredients for the sauce into a saucepan and gently bring to the boil, stirring a little to help the sugar dissolve. Reduce the heat and simmer for eight to 10 minutes. The mixture should look syrupy and will thicken more as it cools. Leave to cool.

Cut the chicken with the grain into 5 x 2cm (2 x ¾in) slices. Remove the softer green bits from the spring onions and trim the tufty base. You need the small bulb and the firmer bits of green for this. Cut the spring onions into 6cm (2½in) lengths. Fold each piece of chicken in half and thread on to wooden or metal skewers, alternating with a piece of spring onion. When they are ready, gently press with the heel of your hand to compact the chicken and neaten the whole skewer.

If cooking on a barbecue, just season the skewers. If cooking on a griddle pan, heat until it's really hot, brush the skewers with oil, then sprinkle with salt. Cook, turning every minute or so, for about seven minutes. Move them around so they cook evenly and adjust the heat as needed.

Now brush the skewers with the sauce and cook for another two or three minutes, turning the skewers every 30 seconds or so and brushing them with sauce. You need to control the heat so the sauce doesn't burn (though a bit of caramelization is good) and the chicken cooks through (check for doneness by cutting into a larger piece). When the chicken is cooked, brush with more teriyaki and sprinkle with togarashi and sesame seeds. Serve with boiled rice, or just salad (the vegetable bit of the Japanese salad on page 126 is good).

pure comfort *dishes to warm and soothe*

chicken with dill and leeks

You might think this recipe comes from Scandinavia – land of dill lovers – but in fact it was inspired by a fish dish I had in Turkey, where whole fish were cooked on a bed of potatoes and dill (and a little raki). You can go the raki route if you prefer. This is a very comforting dish, but light and spring-like at the same time. You need a bit of colour, so serve it with roast tomatoes or a carrot purée. If you're not a dill enthusiast then make this dish with parsley; it's different, but just as good.

SERVES 8

10g (¼oz) dill
75g (2¾oz) unsalted butter,
    slightly softened
2kg (4lb 8oz) chicken
salt and pepper
1 lemon
500g (1lb 2oz) waxy potatoes,
    peeled
4 leeks
400ml (14fl oz) chicken stock
3–4 tbsp dry vermouth
4 tbsp crème fraîche (optional)

Preheat the oven to 200°C/400°F/gas mark 6. Remove the coarser stems from the dill and set them aside. Take the rest of the dill – the light, leafy part – and roughly chop it. Mash the butter with half the chopped dill. Carefully lift the skin of the breast and legs (see page 101) and push under about half the butter. Spread the remaining butter over the bird as well and season with salt and pepper. Put in a roasting tin or a flame- and ovenproof dish from which you can serve the bird. Squeeze the lemon over, then put the shells into the cavity of the bird with the stems of the dill. Truss the chicken, if you like. Cook in the hot oven for 20 minutes.

Slice the potatoes to about the thickness of a pound coin. Wash the leeks, cut off and discard most of the dark green tops and the bases. Chop them into 4cm (1½in) lengths. Wash the chunks of leek thoroughly to ensure you get rid of any soil.

Take the chicken out of the oven and put the potatoes and leeks around it, turning to coat in the juices. Season. Heat the stock to boiling and pour it on to the vegetables with the vermouth. Reduce the oven temperature to 180°C/350°F/gas mark 4 and return the bird to the oven for one hour. The potatoes will become tender and the cooking liquid reduce significantly.

If the vegetables haven't absorbed all the liquid, remove the chicken to a warmed platter and insulate with foil to keep it warm. Set the roasting tin on the hob and boil until the liquid mostly disappears. You can, at this stage, add the crème fraîche (it's entirely a matter of taste, sometimes I do, sometimes I don't). Heat this through – it doesn't have to be completely mixed into the vegetables, there is a rough edge to this dish that makes it all the more satisfying. Check the vegetables for seasoning. Put the bird back on top of the vegetables, throw on the rest of the chopped dill and serve.

chicken loves cream

When French cooking reigned supreme, rivers of cream flowed through my kitchen.
Poulet à l'estragon, carottes forestières, pommes dauphinoise… *these are the dishes
that made me fall in love with restaurants and with cooking. Then the Mediterranean
invaded with all the force of a marauding Roman army and olive oil knocked cream off
its perch. Our eating tastes have changed – now I like Middle Eastern and Vietnamese
food as much as I do French, while* pommes dauphinoise *is an occasional treat – but
I've never stopped cooking those French classics. In fact I had to stop myself from putting
too many creamy bistro dishes in this book.*

*Cream is no longer an expensive ingredient, but it's still luxurious. It has an
extraordinary transformative power and – since it's rich but not overwhelming – it's
perfect with chicken. You might be making a dish that is quite cheap, relatively speaking.
A panful of chicken thighs that you've sautéed with shallots and garlic, deglazing with
white wine and stock. You add fresh peas, broad beans or French beans towards the
end of the cooking time. Of course it's good as it is, but what finishes it off? What turns
it from a nice meal for a Friday night into a dish so good you decide to open a really
good bottle of white to go with it? Cream. It fills the mouth, softens and simultaneously
enriches flavours, makes the ordinary sublime. It also provides a bridge between the
assertive and the subtle. If you think of some of chicken's happiest bedfellows – tarragon,
mustard, Calvados, cheese – cream is what brings them together.*

*Double cream is what I usually go for. It's easy to use as it can be boiled or baked
without splitting (unlike single or whipping cream). Crème fraîche – its tangy French
counterpart – can be boiled, too, though it never seems to give you as thick a sauce when
reduced as double cream. The characteristic sharpness of crème fraîche is great in dishes
where you want acidity as well as richness. It mollifies and heightens, as if you'd added
both cream and lemon. I like it in creamy French sautés, especially those that include
fruit – chicken with prunes or chicken with apples – where there's sweetness that needs
a balancing sharpness.*

*Both double cream and crème fraîche are good for quick chicken suppers, too: you might
sauté a breast, deglaze the pan with vermouth or lemon juice and toss in a handful of
herbs. A slug of cream can pull these elements into a simple but ritzy dish. So a tub of the
stuff is a good ingredient to have in the fridge. It might not look that promising. But it
will always deliver.*

chicken with pumpkin, cream and gruyère

This dish is a duvet, a hug, a totally yielding mixture of soft pumpkin, chicken and melting cheese. And sometimes you need that. It is very rich; small portions are advisable.

SERVES 6

1kg (2lb 4oz) pumpkin or butternut squash (unprepared weight)
3 tbsp olive oil
salt and pepper
8 skinless boneless chicken thighs or breasts
400ml (14fl oz) double cream
1 garlic clove, crushed
25g (scant 1oz) grated Gruyère
25g (scant 1oz) grated Parmesan

Preheat the oven to 200°C/400°F/gas mark 6. Peel and deseed the pumpkin and cut it into wedges. Put the wedges into a roasting tin, brush with olive oil, season and roast in the oven for about 30 minutes, or until completely tender (and even slightly caramelized). Now put the squash into a gratin or other ovenproof dish, one that is big enough to accommodate the chicken too.

Meanwhile, cook the chicken. Simply season it all over, heat 1½ tbsp olive oil in a frying pan and sauté the chicken on both sides until golden and cooked through, eight to 10 minutes. Cut each piece into three. Add the chicken to the pumpkin.

Heat the cream with the garlic until it's boiling, take off the heat, season and pour over the chicken and pumpkin. Sprinkle on both cheeses and bake for 20–25 minutes. The dish should be bubbling and golden. Serve. You need something to cut the richness, so a salad of bitter leaves is good. Children like it with pasta, but I prefer brown rice or another nutty whole grain.

chicken, spinach and cheese polpette

This is a really useful recipe. You can serve these little chicken meatballs with home-made tomato sauce (see page 153, though leave out the cinnamon) and spaghetti, or with plain (unsauced) spaghetti moistened with olive oil, or in bowls of chicken broth (cook small pasta such as orzo, or long-grain rice, in the broth before adding the polpette). And of course you can just stuff them into wraps with lettuce, tomato and mayo, or serve them with some kind of dip. This mixture makes about 50 polpette and I reckon on serving each person eight if I serve them with pasta (they're really not very big); more if I'm just serving them with a dip.

In principle I don't agree with the idea of 'childrens' food', but it's hard to stick to that if you end up with a picky eater in the family. I am always looking for dishes that my nine-year-old will enjoy. And these get the thumbs up. Grown-ups (thankfully) like them just as much.

SERVES 6 (THOUGH IT SLIGHTLY DEPENDS ON HOW YOU SERVE THEM)

500g (1lb 2oz) minced chicken
50g (1¾oz) fresh white or
    brown breadcrumbs
20g (¾oz) grated Parmesan
60g (2oz) grated Gruyère
2–3 tbsp olive oil
½ onion, or 1 small onion, very
    finely chopped
2 garlic cloves, crushed
200g (7oz) spinach
leaves from 3 sprigs of thyme
generous grating of nutmeg
finely grated zest of 1
    unwaxed lemon
salt and pepper

Put the minced chicken in a bowl with the breadcrumbs and the cheeses.

Heat 1 tbsp of the olive oil in a frying pan and sauté the onion over a medium to low heat until soft but not coloured. Add the garlic and cook for another two minutes. Leave to cool.

Put the spinach in a pan with a couple of tbsp of water and cover. Set over a low heat and allow to wilt, turning the leaves over a couple of times. . It will take about four minutes. Drain and leave to cool. Add the cooled onion to the chicken with the thyme, nutmeg, lemon zest and plenty of salt and pepper.

Squeeze the excess water from the spinach and chop it finely. Add to the rest of the ingredients and mix everything with your hands. It's really important that the mixture is well seasoned.

Wet your hands – it makes it easier to shape the polpette – and form the mixture into little balls, about the size of a walnut in its shell. Put them on a tray or baking sheet as you prepare them. If you have time, cover them and chill – it helps them stay firmer – but I often just cook them straight off. Heat 1 tbsp of olive oil in a frying pan and cook the polpette in batches over a medium heat, so the outsides get a good colour, allowing each to form a crust before turning it over. You need to cook and turn the polpette until brown and crusty all over – about three minutes for each batch – then reduce the heat and continue to cook, again turning from time to time, until the polpette are cooked through, roughly another seven minutes (cut into one to check how they're doing; there should be no trace of pink).

chicken with thyme and lemon and smashed garlic potatoes

Very simple but very pretty, especially if you can get your hands on thyme flowers. The chicken also works well with lavender.

The potatoes are fab. I do them in all sorts of versions. You can daub the top of them with crème fraîche (wicked, but good) or add dried chilli flakes or herbs (not to serve with this chicken dish, but with others). It's a 'keeper' recipe.

SERVES 4

FOR THE POTATOES

500g (1lb 2oz) baby waxy potatoes
8 garlic cloves, peeled but left whole, plus 3 garlic cloves, grated
3 tbsp extra virgin olive oil
salt and pepper
leaves from 2 sprigs of thyme

FOR THE CHICKEN

1 small skin-on chicken, jointed into 8, or a mixture of skin-on bone-in joints
4 tbsp extra virgin olive oil
8 sprigs of thyme (and thyme flowers if possible)
finely grated zest of 1 unwaxed lemon, plus the juice of 2

Preheat the oven to 190°C/375°F/gas mark 5. Boil the potatoes in water with the peeled, whole garlic cloves. When the potatoes are just tender, drain them (discard the garlic), put the potatoes into an ovenproof dish and press the top of each so it is a little crushed, but stays in one piece (I use the end of a rolling pin, but a potato masher is good, too). Add the grated garlic, olive oil, salt and pepper and turn the potatoes over in all this. Sprinkle with the thyme.

Put the chicken joints into an ovenproof dish that you can serve from; a cast-iron, enamel or copper dish would be good. They should be able to lie snugly in a single layer. Add the olive oil, salt and pepper and 6 sprigs of thyme (leave some sprigs whole, just use the leaves of others. No need to be exacting about it). Add the zest and juice of one lemon. Throw the squeezed-out shells in too. Toss everything around with your hands. Remove some of the zest of the other lemon with a vegetable peeler and set it aside. Leave all the chicken skin side up and put in the hot oven.

After 10 minutes' cooking, put the potatoes into the oven. They should be roasted for 30 minutes and you need to shake the dish every so often and turn the potatoes over. After the chicken has been in the oven for 30 minutes, add the strips of lemon zest and toss them round in the fat. Cook for a final 10 minutes. Serve the chicken in the dish in which it has been cooked with the leaves from the extra sprigs of thyme and the thyme flowers over the top, with the potatoes.

thyme-roasted chicken with breton onion sauce

This is really old-fashioned and a dream of a dish. I used to make sauce soubise (made from béchamel and puréed onions) from time to time for roast lamb, but never thought of putting an onion sauce with chicken. Then I read about Breton onion sauce (similar to sauce soubise) in one of my favourite cookbooks, Jenny Baker's Cuisine Grandmère (it's out of print but try to track down a copy, it's a gem). She suggested serving it with roast chicken. My Breton sauce is based on her recipe. It's basically a cream-enriched béchamel mixed with a soft, melting mass of cooked onions and a good slug of Calvados.

It's best to back-time the béchamel to be ready just when the chicken has rested. You can do the onion component in advance, but reheating béchamel is always a bit of a pain.

SERVES 6

FOR THE CHICKEN
1.8kg (4lb) chicken
25g (scant 1oz) unsalted butter
leaves from 4 sprigs of thyme
salt and pepper

FOR THE ONIONS
30g (1oz) unsalted butter,
    slightly softened
450g (1lb) onions, finely
    chopped

FOR THE SAUCE
300ml (½ pint) whole milk
slice of onion
a few parsley stalks
4 black peppercorns
1 bay leaf
30g (1oz) unsalted butter
30g (1oz) plain flour
a little grated nutmeg
3 tbsp crème fraîche
1 tsp Dijon mustard
2 tbsp Calvados

Preheat the oven to 180°C/350°F/gas mark 4. Start with the chicken. Mash the butter with the thyme, salt and pepper. Carefully loosen the skin over the breast (see page 101). Using your fingers, spread about half of the butter under the skin, without tearing it. Now spread the remainder on the outside of the bird, season and put into a roasting tin. Cook in the hot oven for 1 hour 15 minutes, basting every so often.

Now prepare the onions (you can do these ahead of time). Melt the butter in a heavy-based pan and add the onions. Turn them over to coat in the butter, add 2 tbsp of water and cover. Cook over a very low heat until completely soft, being careful not to let them brown. Keep an eye on them, adding a spoonful of water every so often. They will sweat to a lovely sweet softness.

When the chicken is cooked allow it to rest, covered in foil, for 15 minutes.

To make the sauce put the milk, onion, parsley, peppercorns and bay leaf in a saucepan and slowly bring to just under the boil. Take off the heat and leave for 20 minutes to infuse.

Melt the butter in a heavy-based saucepan, add the flour and stir over a medium-low heat for a minute. Take off the heat. Strain in the milk, a little at a time, stirring until smooth. Season and add the nutmeg. Return to the heat and stir until boiling. Reduce the heat and simmer for three minutes. Add the onions with their juices, the crème fraîche, mustard and Calvados and taste for seasoning. Pour into a warm jug. Serve the chicken, its juices and the sauce. Simple accompaniments – French beans or Savoy cabbage, waxy potatoes – are best.

soothing north indian chicken

This is not one of those head-spinningly rich or complexly spiced Indian dishes; it's simple and modest, sort of the Indian equivalent of chicken soup or shepherd's pie. It needs something soothing on the side, such as dal, or greens fried with ginger and garlic.

SERVES 4

8 skinless bone-in chicken thighs
2 tbsp ghee or groundnut oil
2 tsp cumin seeds
½ tsp pepper
1 large onion, grated
8 garlic cloves, grated
30g (1oz) root ginger, peeled and grated
1 tbsp coriander seeds, toasted and ground (see page 66)
1 red chilli, halved, deseeded and sliced
1 green chilli, halved, deseeded and sliced
4 tbsp plain yogurt
good squeeze of lime juice
1 tsp soft light brown sugar (optional)
salt
small bunch of coriander, roughly chopped

Put the chicken into a saucepan, pour in 500ml (18fl oz) of water and bring to the boil. Immediately reduce the heat so the water is gently simmering, cover and cook for 35 minutes, or until the chicken is just cooked through. Lift the chicken out with a slotted spoon and set aside. Measure the cooking liquid and add enough water to make it up to 500ml (18fl oz) once more.

Rinse out the saucepan, dry it, then heat the ghee or groundnut oil in it over a medium heat. Add the cumin seeds and pepper and cook for 30 seconds, then add the grated onion, garlic and ginger. Cook until the mixture is soft and pale gold, a matter of seven or eight minutes, then add the ground coriander seeds and both chillies. Cook for another two minutes, then reduce the heat and stir in the yogurt. Now stir in the reserved cooking liquor, adding a little at a time.

Return the chicken to the pot, increase the heat so the chicken is hot right through, then reduce the heat once more and simmer for about four minutes. Don't boil the mixture.

Add the lime juice and sugar (if using) and season with salt. Taste to check the seasoning. Throw in the coriander and heat for 15 seconds so it can start to release its fragrance. Serve immediately.

chicken pot-roasted in milk, bay and nutmeg

I've never been keen on the Italian dish of pork cooked in milk, but I was convinced to try this by Faith Durand who runs www.thekitchn.com website in the States. She heard about it from Jamie Oliver and made some adjustments, and I have made my own. Faith thinks it is the best chicken recipe in the world and my children would be inclined to agree with her. You won't believe me until you try it, but it is a great dish: the chicken stays completely succulent and becomes sweet, imbued with and enriched by the flavourings in the milk. The nutmeggy milk makes it a bit like eating roast chicken with bread sauce (but without the hassle of making bread sauce). One of the most comforting dishes you could wish for.

SERVES 6

25g (scant 1oz) unsalted butter
2 tbsp olive oil
salt and pepper
1.8kg (4lb) chicken
350ml (12fl oz) whole milk
10 garlic cloves, peeled but left whole
3 bay leaves
good grating of nutmeg
finely grated zest of 2 unwaxed lemons

Preheat the oven to 180°C/350°F/gas mark 4. Heat the butter and olive oil in a pan that can hold the chicken and has a lid. Season the bird, tie the legs together if you want and brown it all over, using two big forks or wooden spoons to turn the chicken, seasoning it as you go. Try to avoid piercing the skin. Pour off the fat; you don't need to throw it out, you can keep it to fry potatoes.

Add the milk, garlic, bay leaves, nutmeg and lemon zest to the pot. Bring to just under the boil, then remove from the heat. Put a lid on the pot and cook in the hot oven for 1½ hours, removing the lid halfway through cooking. Baste occasionally, spooning the milk up over the bird.

At the end of cooking time the bird will be succulent and golden and the juices will be copious and slightly curdled. Squash the garlic cloves with the back of a fork so they break down and flavour the juices. Taste; you may want to add a little more nutmeg.

Serve – I love it with orzo or a rice pilaf – spooning the juices over the chicken and whatever starch you choose for a side dish. The vegetable you choose depends on the time of year. In winter it's good with roast carrots, in the summer roast tomatoes and a salad of bitter leaves.

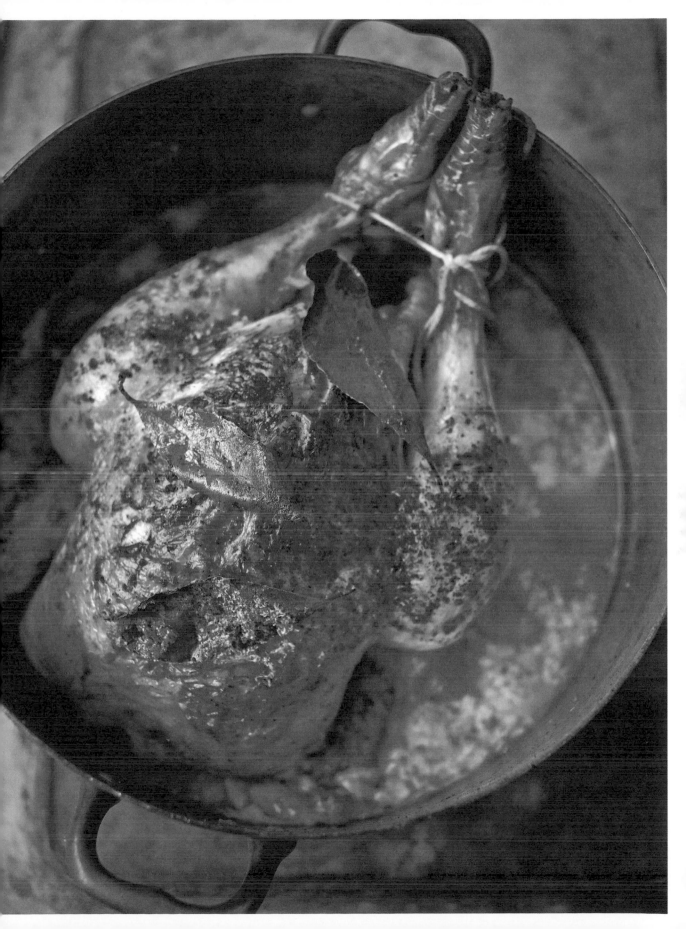

hot and sweet lime chicken wings

Hot, burnished and sticky, this is barbecue food without the barbecue. These are great in the summer when you can't be bothered to put the barbecue on and just as good at Hallowe'en or Guy Fawkes bonfire parties. Push the chilli quota higher if you want to.

SERVES 4

finely grated zest of 6 limes, plus the juice of 8, plus lime wedges to serve

4 red chillies, finely sliced (don't remove the seeds)

2 green chillies, deseeded and finely sliced

8 garlic cloves, crushed

290g (10¼oz) lime marmalade

100g (3½oz) dark soft brown sugar

4cm (1½in) root ginger, peeled and very finely chopped

20 chicken wings

roughly chopped coriander, to serve

soured cream or Greek yogurt, to serve

Mix all the ingredients except the chicken, coriander and soured cream in a bowl, pressing the marmalade with the back of a spoon to break it down. Put the chicken wings into this and turn them all over with your hands, making sure they get well coated. Cover and marinate in the fridge for a couple of hours. Bring to room temperature before cooking.

When you're ready to cook, preheat the oven to 210°C/410°F/gas mark 6½. Lay the chicken wings in a single layer in a couple of roasting tins (if you put them on top of each other, they will sweat rather than brown). Cook in the hot oven for 40 minutes, turning them over halfway through. If they are getting too dark in colour (because of the sugars burning), cover them with foil.

Sprinkle with coriander and serve on a big platter with a plain green salad, or an avocado and leaf salad, and rice. Lime wedges – chargrilled or fresh – look great on the platter, too. Offer little bowls of soured cream or Greek yogurt to temper the heat.

chicken loves fruit

Some friends have commented (thus risking the end of invitations from me to supper) that I really want two desserts, starting with the main course. This is because of my love of fruit. It isn't just that I find the flavour of meat and fruit together irresistible – I am so bewitched by it you would think I had either Moroccan or Persian blood in my veins – I also love dealing with fruit. Its ripeness, its fecundity, its colour. And I love the sense of the medieval and the exotic that fruit and meat together confers. Persian khoreshes and Moroccan tajines – in which the pairing of meat and fruit is a main characteristic – seem as if they are from another time and a magical, far away place. And it's a blend we British love. Christmas pudding was initially a potage of meat and dried fruit. We love roast pork and apple sauce, roast lamb with quince jelly (combinations that make the French roll their eyes, but that a Catalan – with his Arab influenced sweet-savoury cuisine – completely understands).

Pork and lamb are more obvious stablemates for fruit. The sweetness of fruit chimes with that of their meat and fat but, crucially, is balanced by the fruit's tart quality. You can't, however, throw apple sauce at roast chicken (though I do eat roast chicken with a vinegar-laced quince or apple jelly). Chicken isn't sweet (though caramelize the skin during browning and you're creating a bit of that), so you need a 'bridge' to make sure the end result isn't sickly. If you can establish one – and Moroccan, Persian and even some Indian, Thai and British dishes do – then chicken and fruit is surprisingly good. In a chicken and quince tajine, the bridge is provided by sweet and earthy spices such as ginger, cumin, saffron and cinnamon. In a salad of chicken and cherries it's the tarragon – good with both chicken and cherries – that enables the coupling. A braise of chicken and apples uses cream and cider as the bridge. (Sometimes a recipe will suggest you can replace the cider with apple juice. You can't. The cider gives a yeasty, rugged base which is a foil for the sweetness of the apples and yet echoes them.) Recipes for this dish often suggest frying slices of apple at the end until they caramelize at the edges, but the apples must be a tart variety, such as Granny Smith. Use a bland and sweet Golden Delicious and you've lost the point.

There's chicken with cherries, peaches, apricots, apples, pears, oranges, mangoes and prunes in this book. If you're not a fruit lover you might find it hard to believe that they work, but they do. A few are gentle, some are mouth-puckeringly fresh, most are luscious. Rhubarb hasn't made it, but only because I couldn't squeeze it in. Think that's a step too far? The Danes know how to cook chicken with rhubarb. But that's a delicious story for another time...

chicken with leeks, apples and cider

This is my partner's favourite dish (and the first thing I ever cooked for him) so it's quite special to me. Perfect comfort food. Although it could just as easily come from Cornwall or Devon (because of the cider), it really takes me to Normandy.

SERVES 4

salt and pepper
8 skin-on bone-in chicken thighs, or a mixture of joints
40g (1½oz) unsalted butter
700g (1lb 9oz) leeks
2 dessert apples
1 tbsp plain flour
500ml (18fl oz) dry cider
6 sprigs of thyme, plus leaves from 2 more sprigs to serve
150ml (5fl oz) double cream
1 tsp caster sugar

Season the chicken pieces and heat 25g (scant 1oz) of the butter in a large sauté pan (one which has a lid) or a wide casserole. Brown the chicken on both sides and then set the pieces aside while you cook the leeks. (Make sure not to burn the butter.)

Remove the tough outer leaves from the leeks. Trim the bases and cut off the tough, very dark leaves at the top. Wash the leeks really well, making sure that you get rid of any soil that is lodged in them. Cut into about 3cm (1¼in) lengths. Add the leeks to the fat in the pan in which you cooked the chicken and sauté without browning for about 10 minutes; they should soften but not become sloppy.

Meanwhile, peel one of the apples, halve and cut into wedges. Melt the remaining butter in a small frying pan and gently brown the wedges on each side. Leave until you need them.

Add the flour to the leeks and turn them over in the juices. Continue to cook for a couple of minutes. Take the pan off the heat and slowly add the cider, stirring all the time. Return to the heat, bring to the boil, then add the chicken, sprigs of thyme and the sautéed apple (don't wash the apple pan). Immediately reduce the heat to a simmer, put the lid on and leave to cook over a low heat for about 35 minutes. The chicken should be cooked through, with no trace of pink.

Lift the chicken pieces out of the casserole and simmer the cooking juices until reduced by about one-third. Add the cream, bring to the boil and cook for a couple of minutes.

Peel and cut the other apple into wedges and put in the frying pan in which you cooked the first apple. Sauté gently, adding the caster sugar to help the slices caramelize nicely on the outside. Cook until the apple slices are tender. Return the chicken to the sauce and heat gently. At the last minute, add the newly sautéed apples, sprinkle with the thyme leaves and serve.

bird in a pot

The idea of a poached or pot-roast chicken isn't sexy. But I was surprised as I tried recipes, both old and new, how much friends loved these dishes. A poached bird is succulent and comes with copious juices, while herb relish, or crème fraîche mixed with shallots and capers, can embellish.

Pot-roasting gives a more intense 'sauce' and a perfectly moist bird. You need to cook gently and keep an eye on the moisture levels, but pot-roasts require only minimal attention.

There are lots of hit-you-in-the-face flavours in this book, plenty of griddled flesh and dishes you can cook in a hurry. But don't ignore the gentle, the subtle and the slow.

pot-roast chicken with figs

Pot-roast chicken often seems like a pure, 'clean' sort of meal, not a luxurious one. This, however, because of the figs, honey and Armagnac, is quite grand, more than a little special.

SERVES 6

1½ tbsp olive oil

salt and pepper

1.8kg (4lb) chicken

1 large onion, roughly
   chopped

2 tbsp Armagnac

125ml (4fl oz) dry white wine

125ml (4fl oz) chicken stock

4 sprigs of thyme

1 bay leaf

18 figs, stalks snipped, halved

1 tbsp cider vinegar

2 tbsp honey

20g (¾oz) cold unsalted butter,
   cut into cubes

Preheat the oven to 180°C/350°F/gas mark 4. Heat the olive oil, season the chicken and brown it all over. Remove the chicken.

Pour off all but 1½ tbsp of the fat from the pan and cook the onion in this over a medium heat until soft and golden. Deglaze the pan with the Armagnac, scraping with a wooden spoon to remove all the sticky bits, then add the wine, stock, thyme and bay leaf. Add a good grinding of black pepper.

Return the chicken and any juices that have run out of it. Cover, put into the oven and cook for 70 minutes, then take the lid off and cook for another 20 minutes. Baste every so often. Strain off the cooking juices. Cover the chicken to keep warm.

Skim the fat from the cooking juices. Put the juices into a frying pan (one that will hold the figs in a single layer) and boil to reduce them. You want a liquid that is slightly syrupy. Reduce the heat and add the figs, vinegar and honey, to flavour the juices and make the figs tender and glossy, about four minutes. Remove the figs with a slotted spoon and whisk in the cold butter gradually; it makes the sauce rich and shiny.

Serve the chicken – either whole or jointed – on a warm platter with the figs around it and the sauce in a heated jug on the side.

poule au pot with caper and shallot cream

Leave out the chicken livers from the stuffing if you prefer, but if so increase the amount of bacon by 50g (1¾oz). You don't have to serve the cream sauce and it isn't authentic, just something I do myself. A pot of Dijon mustard suffices, or go Italian and serve with Salsa verde (see page 142).

SERVES 6

FOR THE STUFFING
15g (½oz) unsalted butter
150g (5½oz) bacon, chopped
1 small onion, finely chopped
2 garlic cloves, finely chopped
2 chicken livers, chopped
60g (2oz) fresh breadcrumbs
1 small egg, lightly beaten
handful of chopped parsley
good grating of fresh nutmeg
finely grated zest of ½ lemon

FOR THE CHICKEN
1.4kg (3lb 3½oz) chicken
3 leeks
1 celery stick
3 sprigs of thyme
small bunch of parsley stalks
2 bay leaves
8 black peppercorns
1 onion, quartered
12 slim carrots, peeled
1.5 litres (2 pints 13fl oz)
    chicken stock, or water
about 12 small waxy potatoes

FOR THE SAUCE
juice of ½ lemon
300ml (½ pint) double cream
leaves from 2 sprigs of
    tarragon, chopped
2 tsp finely chopped parsley
3 tbsp capers, rinsed
2 small shallots, finely chopped
2 tbsp extra virgin olive oil

To make the stuffing, melt the butter in a frying pan and add the bacon and onion. Sauté until the onion is soft and pale gold. Add the garlic and chicken livers and cook for a couple of minutes more. Put into a bowl, add all the other ingredients and season well.

Remove the fat from round the cavity of the chicken and stuff it, sewing it up with a poultry needle, or using a couple of skewers to keep it secure. Tie up the chicken legs to keep the shape neat (not essential but it does look better).

Remove the coarser outer leaves from the leeks and cut off the dark tops and trim the bases. Cut into 6cm (2½in) lengths and wash thoroughly to remove any trapped soil.

Cut the celery in half and tie it in a bundle with the thyme, parsley stalks and bay leaves to make a nice fat bouquet garni. Put this into a pot with the chicken, peppercorns, quartered onion, carrots and stock or water. Bring to the boil, then immediately reduce the heat, cover and cook really gently for 1½ hours. Fifteen minutes before the end of cooking time, add the leeks and boil the potatoes (I like to cook the potatoes separately or they make the broth cloudy). Remove the onion and the bouquet garni.

To make the sauce, add the lemon juice to the cream – it will thicken as you stir it in – then add everything else. Check for seasoning and balance.

A whole chicken that's been poached – without browning – isn't a thing of beauty, so I tend to remove the meat and put it on a platter with the vegetables and stuffing and provide a big jug of the broth (or you can prepare a single plate for each person). I like it best served in soup plates (there's room for the broth). Offer the creamy sauce, or whatever sauce you want to serve, and some Dijon mustard on the side.

chicken in the pot with vegetables and barley

It sounds very plain, but this is one of the best things I cook. It's like a very substantial version of the chicken soup my family grew up with. My mum adds boiled potatoes to the finished dish. You can spoon on buttermilk or cream, too, or offer mustard on the side.

SERVES 6

4 leeks
300g (10½oz) long slim carrots,
    preferably with greenery
1½ tbsp olive oil
1 medium-sized chicken
    (about 1.6kg/3lb 8oz)
salt and pepper
1 onion, finely chopped
2 celery sticks, finely chopped
bouquet garni, plus more
    parsley stalks
200ml (7fl oz) dry vermouth
55g (2oz) pearl barley
about 4 tbsp chopped flat-leaf
    parsley leaves

Remove the discoloured outer layers from the leeks and trim the dark tops. Cut them into 4cm (1½in) lengths and wash thoroughly under running water to remove any trapped soil. Trim the carrots (if you've bought them in a bunch leave a little of the tufty top on each). Wash really well, but don't peel. If you have fatter carrots, cut them in halves or quarters lengthways.

Heat the olive oil in a heavy-based casserole over a medium heat and brown the chicken on all sides. I use wooden spoons to help me turn it over. Try not to tear the skin while you're doing this and season as you go. Remove the chicken, set it aside and add the onion and celery to the pot. Sauté gently until the onion is softening but isn't coloured, about five minutes. Return the chicken and add the bouquet garni, parsley stalks, carrots, a good grinding of black pepper, the vermouth and 800ml (1 pint 7fl oz) of water.

Bring to the boil, then immediately reduce the heat right down, cover and poach the chicken for 1½ hours. The water must not boil; it has to be gentle or the chicken will become tough. When the chicken has 45 minutes of cooking time left, add the barley. When there are 15 minutes left, add the leeks. At the end, add the chopped parsley.

Serve in big broad soup plates, giving each person some of the vegetables, barley, broth and chicken. My mum serves boiled potatoes with this, which you can break up in your broth, or buttered wheaten (soda) bread. I must admit to gilding the lily a little (well, why not?) and offer cream, mustard and – sometimes – even horseradish. It also goes well with the accompaniments you serve with Little(ish) bollito misto (see page 142), though of course that's not remotely authentic.

pot-roast chicken with bacon, baby gems and creamy parsley sauce

Even though it's a pot-roast, this is a very elegant dish. The baby gems – with their lovely milky centres – become soft but retain bite. Excellent spring eating.

SERVES 6–8

salt and pepper
1.8kg (4lb) chicken
5 baby gem lettuces
25g (scant 1oz) unsalted butter
1 tbsp olive oil
350ml (12fl oz) dry white wine
4 sprigs of thyme
150g (5½oz) bacon lardons
200ml (7fl oz) double cream
3 tbsp finely chopped flat-leaf
    parsley leaves
good squeeze of lemon juice

Preheat the oven to 170°C/340°F/gas mark 3½. Season the chicken inside and out. Remove any discoloured outer leaves from the lettuces and trim the root ends.

Heat the butter and oil in a reasonably heavy-based, ovenproof saucepan or casserole in which the chicken can sit snugly surrounded by the lettuces. It needs to have a lid. Brown the chicken all over – carefully turning it so you don't rip the skin – then pour in the wine and add the thyme. Bring to the boil then immediately reduce the heat, cover and put into the oven.

Cook for 1½ hours, taking the lid off after 50 minutes and tucking the baby gems in round the bird. Baste them with the cooking juices to make sure they are well moistened.

Brown the lardons in a small frying pan in their own fat – it will just start to run out when you heat them – and scatter them over the top of the lettuces. Return to the oven without the lid. Continue to cook, basting the lettuces and turning them every so often. The chicken is cooked when – if you pierce between the legs and the rest of the body with the tip of a sharp knife – the juices run clear with no trace of pink.

Take the chicken and the lettuces out of the pot (be careful with the lettuces as they are delicate), put on a warmed platter, cover with foil and insulate (I use old tea towels for this). Remove the thyme and strain out the bacon (reserve it). Pour the cooking juices into a jug, skim the fat from the top and discard it. Heat the cooking juices and add the cream. Boil until you have a sauce about the thickness of single cream, then add the parsley and reserved bacon. Add a squeeze of lemon juice (this will thicken the sauce) and taste for seasoning. Serve the chicken on a platter surrounded by the lettuce with the creamy parsley sauce on the side.

chicken, spinach and cauliflower risotto with melting fontina

This is a bit like the Sunday lunch I used to enjoy as a child – roast chicken, cauliflower cheese and greens – but all mixed together in a soft bowlful. If you can't find fontina, use Gruyère instead. It's different – it doesn't melt in the same way and fontina is richer – but it's not a bad substitute.

SERVES 2–3

½ tbsp olive oil
10g (¼oz) unsalted butter
1 small onion, finely chopped
600ml (1 pint) chicken stock
150g (5½oz) risotto rice
50ml (2fl oz) dry white wine
   or dry vermouth
½ medium cauliflower, broken
   into florets
75g (2¾oz) spinach leaves,
   washed, coarse stems
   removed
100g (3½oz) cooked chicken,
   torn into pieces
freshly grated nutmeg
45g (1¾oz) fontina cheese,
   coarsely grated
salt and pepper
grated Parmesan, to serve
   (optional)

Heat the olive oil and butter in a heavy-based saucepan and gently sauté the onion until it is soft but not coloured. Heat the chicken stock separately, so it is gently simmering.

Add the rice to the onion and stir it around in the butter. Cook for a couple of minutes over a medium heat, then add the wine or vermouth. Let this bubble until it has almost disappeared, stirring all the time. Now add the stock, a ladleful at a time, again stirring the rice constantly. Only add a new ladleful of stock when the previous one has been absorbed. It will take about 25 minutes for the rice to cook; it should end up soft but with a little bite still in the centre of each grain.

Before the cooking time is up – when there's about 10 minutes left – boil or microwave the cauliflower (I microwave both cauliflower and broccoli, I think it's a great method for them) until only just tender. Add this to the risotto and keep stirring, being careful not to crush the cauliflower. When there are about three minutes left to go, add the spinach, chicken and nutmeg. Stir in the cheese right at the end (it will melt in the heat) and add salt and pepper to taste (you probably won't need much salt as reduced stock makes risotto salty). Serve immediately. You can offer some grated Parmesan on the side if you want, but it is pretty strong already.

remains of the day *what to do with the rest of that bird...*

chicken and pumpkin laksa

There are many different kinds of laksa – essentially a thick noodle soup – and it varies from country to country (it's found in Malaysia, Indonesia, Singapore and Cambodia). This is a simple version, perfect for cooking midweek (it's pretty quick, despite having to do a bit of pounding to make the paste) and a great vehicle for leftover chicken. You can add other ingredients (beansprouts, beans, peppers), it depends on what you have. I'm usually quite purist about dishes (I don't like mucking about with classics) but on a Wednesday night, when you're hungry and short of time, I think anything goes. You can use wide rice noodles or, if it's all you have, rice vermicelli.

SERVES 4

450g (1lb) pumpkin,
　　unprepared weight
2 bird's eye chillies
2 lemon grass stalks
4 garlic cloves, roughly
　　chopped
2cm (¾in) root ginger, peeled
　　and finely chopped
good knob of virgin coconut
　　oil or 1 tbsp of any other oil
　　you like, plus more to blend
　　the paste (optional)
bunch of coriander
finely grated zest and juice of
　　1 lime, or to taste
½ small onion, sliced into thin
　　wedges
600ml (1 pint) chicken stock
400ml can of coconut milk
2 tbsp fish sauce, or to taste
100g (3½oz) cherry tomatoes,
　　halved
75g (2¾oz) dried rice noodles
250g (9oz) cooked chicken,
　　torn into pieces (you can add
　　more if you have it)
big handful – literally – of
　　baby spinach leaves
handful of mint leaves, torn

Halve, deseed and peel the pumpkin then cut the flesh into chunks about 2.5cm (1in) square. Put these into a steamer and cook over boiling water for about 15 minutes. The pieces should be tender.

Slit the chillies along their length; you can decide whether to remove the seeds or not (I don't). Chop. Remove the tougher outer leaves from the lemon grass and roughly chop the paler hearts. Put the chillies, lemon grass, garlic and ginger into a small food processor (or a mortar and pestle) and whizz or pound until you have a rough paste. If you're using a food processor you might need to add a little coconut or rapeseed oil to help it blend. Add the coriander stalks and half the leaves, both chopped, and the lime zest and pound or blitz again.

Heat the good knob of coconut or rapeseed oil in a saucepan and add the onion. Cook gently until it softens a little but is still pale in colour. Add the spice paste. Cook over a medium heat for another minute or so, until you can smell that the spices are no longer 'raw'. Add the stock and coconut milk and bring to just under the boil. Add the fish sauce and the tomatoes and simmer gently for about seven minutes (the tomatoes don't have to get soft; they should keep their shape).

Prepare the noodles according to the packet instructions.

Add the pumpkin, chicken and spinach to the laksa and allow the pumpkin and chicken to warm through thoroughly and the spinach to wilt. Finally, stir in the rest of the coriander leaves, chopped, the mint and the lime juice. Taste for seasoning and balance (you might want more lime juice or fish sauce). Divide the noodles between four bowls and ladle the laksa on top.

vietnamese chicken and sweet potato curry

It's great to have a dish as flavourful as this on the table in around 20 minutes. And made with leftovers, too… (what could be better?)

SERVES 4

1 tbsp rapeseed or groundnut oil, or any other oil you prefer
2 onions, halved and cut into crescent moon-shaped slices
2 red chillies, halved, deseeded and shredded
1 tbsp ground coriander
½ tbsp turmeric
2 x 160ml cans of coconut cream
200ml (7fl oz) chicken stock
1 tbsp fish sauce
1½ tbsp soft light brown sugar
600g (1lb 5oz) sweet potato, peeled and cubed
800g (1lb 12oz) cooked chicken, torn into pieces
juice of 1 lime
salt and pepper
handful of basil leaves, torn

Heat the oil and cook the onions over a medium heat until pale gold. Add the chillies and ground spices and cook for another minute, stirring a little. Add the coconut cream, stock, fish sauce, sugar and sweet potato. Bring to just under the boil, then reduce the heat and cook until the sweet potato is tender (about 15 minutes).

Add the chicken to the curry. Cook for another two minutes or so, or until the chicken is warmed through and the sweet potato is completely soft. To thicken the dish, press some of the sweet potato with the back of a wooden spoon so it disintegrates into the sauce. Add the lime juice, check the seasoning and stir in the basil. Serve with boiled rice.

chicken, fennel and pancetta gratin

Okay, I am not reinventing the wheel here. In terms of using leftovers this is about as simple and old-fashioned as you can get, but it's easy and satisfying. Make sure you season the sauce properly, that's key; you might need to add a little bit more mustard than stipulated. It's very easy to adapt this recipe too: replace the fennel with blanched broccoli or leeks, or add a layer of spinach.

SERVES 4

3 fennel bulbs
75g (2¾oz) pancetta, cut into chunks, or bacon lardons
15g (½oz) unsalted butter
3 tbsp plain flour
100ml (3½fl oz) dry white wine
250ml (9fl oz) whole milk
½ tsp English mustard, or to taste
salt and pepper
85g (3oz) grated Parmesan
2 tbsp double cream (optional)
375g (13oz) cooked chicken, torn into pieces

Trim the fennel bulbs (reserve any little feathery fronds) and remove any tough outer leaves. Quarter and remove the core in each piece. Cook the fennel – microwave, steam or boil in a little water – until it has lost its hardness but is not tender all the way through. Drain really well. Sauté the pancetta or bacon in its own fat. Preheat the oven to 190°C/375°F/gas mark 5.

Make a white sauce by melting the butter and stirring in the flour to form a roux. Cook over a low heat for a couple of minutes, then take off the heat and start adding the wine a little drop at a time, stirring well after each addition to make sure the liquid is well incorporated and the mixture is lump free. Gradually add the milk in the same way. Return to the heat and bring to the boil, stirring all the time. The sauce will thicken. Once it is boiling, reduce the heat and let it simmer for about four minutes to cook the flour. Add the mustard, seasoning and Parmesan and, once the cheese has melted, the cream (if using).

Lay the fennel in a gratin dish, season, then top with the chicken, bacon and any little fennel fronds you collected. Pour the sauce over the top and bake in the hot oven for 20 minutes, or until bubbling and golden. Serve immediately.

chicken, date and lentil brown rice pilaf with saffron butter

I can't tell you how often I make a pilaf using this recipe as a blueprint. When I don't have that much chicken, I sauté an aubergine to extend the 'meatiness'. If I'm being careful about carbs, I leave out the dates. If I don't feel like saffron, I add shredded bits of preserved lemon to the pilaf and eat it with plain yogurt. Whatever you do, it always ends up greater than the sum of its parts. Pretty luxurious for a dish based on leftovers.

SERVES 6

15g (½oz) unsalted butter,
  plus 30g (1oz) more for the
  saffron butter
1 onion, finely chopped
2 garlic cloves, finely chopped
300g (10½oz) brown basmati
  rice, washed until the water
  runs clear
700ml (1¼ pints) chicken stock
12 dates, pitted and cut into
  thin slices, lengthways
finely grated zest of 1 orange
  and juice of ½
200g (7oz) Puy lentils, rinsed
salt and pepper
good squeeze of lemon juice
1 tbsp olive oil
350g (12oz) cooked chicken,
  torn into pieces
25g (scant 1oz) chopped,
  unsalted pistachios or
  toasted flaked almonds
4 tbsp roughly chopped
  coriander leaves
generous pinch of saffron
  strands
300g (10½oz) Greek yogurt

Heat the 15g (½oz) of butter in a heavy-based saucepan and sauté the onion until soft and pale gold. Add the garlic and cook for another couple of minutes. Now add the rice and stir it around until it is well coated in the butter and just beginning to toast. Add the chicken stock, dates and orange zest and bring to the boil. Reduce the heat, cover the pan and cook for about 30 minutes. The stock will become absorbed in this time; if the rice gets too dry, add a little boiling water.

At the same time, cook the lentils in plenty of boiling water until tender (the lentils are cooked separately because the cooking time can be different from that of the rice, also the lentils make their cooking liquid murky, which doesn't look so good). The lentils can take anything from 15–30 minutes to become tender, depending on their age, but be very careful not to overcook them. They need to retain their shape and can very quickly turn to mush. Once the lentils are cooked, drain, rinse in hot water and add to the rice. Fork through, season with salt and pepper and add a good squeeze of lemon juice.

Heat the olive oil in a frying pan and quickly reheat the cooked chicken. Season. Gently fork the chicken into the cooked rice and lentils along with the nuts, coriander and orange juice. The dish should be moist but not 'wet'. Taste the dish for seasoning.

Quickly make the saffron butter: melt the 30g (1oz) butter in a pan, add the saffron and stir to help it colour the butter.

Put the rice into a broad shallow bowl, spoon on some yogurt (serve the rest on the side) then pour on the saffron butter. Serve immediately. You don't want anything complicated on the side (there's enough going on in this dish). A spinach or watercress salad (add cucumber for crunch) would be perfect.

chicken, leek and pea speltotto with vermouth

There are two ways you can go when it comes to leftovers. You can be frugal and restrained – the freekeh with roast vegetable recipe (see page 215) uses this approach – or you can go luxurious. This speltotto is such a dish. It takes very humble ingredients and enriches them with a bit of cream and a slosh of vermouth. (You can leave the cream out if you are watching your fat intake. It will be less luxurious, but still good.)

Using spelt – which is a healthy alternative – produces a less creamy risotto than arborio rice, but on the up side, it doesn't need to be stirred constantly.

SERVES 2–3

2 leeks, coarse outer leaves removed, trimmed
knob of unsalted butter
½ tbsp olive oil
2 shallots, finely chopped
150g (5½oz) spelt
50ml (2fl oz) dry vermouth
300ml (½ pint) chicken stock, plus more if needed
50g (1¾oz) frozen peas
100g (3½oz) cooked chicken, torn into pieces
3 tbsp crème fraîche or double cream
leaves from a couple of sprigs of tarragon (optional)
¼ tbsp finely chopped parsley leaves, or a bit more if you don't have any tarragon
grated Parmesan or pecorino, to serve

Cut the leeks into rings about 5cm (2in) thick and wash really well. Drain. Heat the butter and olive oil in a saucepan, add the leeks and shallots and cook over a medium heat for about four minutes. Tip in the spelt and stir it round so that it gets coated in all the cooking juices. Add the vermouth and let it simmer away until you only have a few spoonfuls left.

Meanwhile, heat the chicken stock and leave it simmering on a low heat. Add this to the risotto in ladelfuls, only adding new stuff when the previous lot has been absorbed. You need to keep adding stock and stirring (not constantly, but fairly frequently) until all the stock is used up and the spelt is tender (there will still be a little 'bite' in the centre of each grain). Add more stock or boiling water if you run out of liquid. It will take about 25 minutes for the spelt to become tender. Stir in the frozen peas five minutes before the end of cooking time.

Add the chicken and crème fraîche and cook until it has heated right through. Add the herbs, cook for another minute, check the seasoning, then serve with the grated Parmesan or pecorino.

cavatelli with chicken, pancetta, peas and cream

One of the easiest things you can do with cold roast chicken. If you have a few spoonfuls of gravy then put that in, too, with the cream. It will make the dish rather beige in colour but is gorgeously enriching.

You can use any pasta shape for this, I just particularly like cavatelli, (trofie are good, too). This is a brilliant Sunday or Monday night supper.

SERVES 4

225g (8oz) cavatelli pasta
15g (½oz) unsalted butter
1 small onion, finely chopped
70g (2½oz) pancetta, cut into cubes
3 garlic cloves, finely chopped
200g (7oz) cooked chicken, torn into pieces
175g (6oz) frozen peas
250ml (9fl oz) double cream
finely grated zest of ½ unwaxed lemon
salt and pepper
leaves from 6 sprigs of mint, roughly torn, or 1 tbsp chopped flat-leaf parsley leaves
freshly grated Parmesan, to serve

Boil the pasta in plenty of water until al dente.

Make the sauce while the pasta is cooking. Melt the butter in a frying pan and gently sauté the onion and pancetta until they are soft and golden. Add the garlic and cook for another two minutes, then add the chicken, peas, cream and lemon zest. Season and bring just to the boil, then reduce the heat, add the herbs and allow everything to meld for a minute or so (the herbs flavour the cream during this time).

Drain the pasta and return it to the saucepan in which it was cooked, adding the sauce. Taste the whole thing and adjust the seasoning. Pour into a warmed serving dish and serve with some Parmesan thrown over the top. Offer more Parmesan on the side.

bird pie

There's nothing like a pie. It might look as though this is a very thick white sauce. It is. The leeks, once they're added, can make the filling quite liquid as they continue to cook and you're also adding lemon juice and cream, so the base sauce needs to be thick.

SERVES 6

60g (2oz) unsalted butter

60g (2oz) plain flour, plus
more to dust

500ml (18fl oz) whole milk

salt and pepper

3 tsp Dijon mustard, plus
more to taste

juice of ½ lemon, plus more
to taste

3 tbsp capers, rinsed

leaves from a small bunch of
parsley, finely chopped

3 tbsp crème fraîche

3 medium leeks, bases
removed, cut into rings
and washed

450g (1lb) cooked chicken,
torn or cut into pieces

300g (10½oz) puff pastry

2 egg yolks, beaten with
2 tsp milk

Heat 40g (1½oz) of the butter in a saucepan and add the flour. Stir this over a medium-low heat for a minute. Remove from the heat and start adding the milk a little at a time (it's better if the milk has been heated, but often I don't have time).

Mix well with a wooden spoon to ensure there are no lumps; the mixture must be smooth. Keep adding and stirring until all the milk has been added. Season. Return the pan to the heat and, stirring continuously, bring to the boil. The mixture will thicken considerably. Once it has come to the boil, reduce the heat and simmer for about three minutes (this 'cooks' the flour in the sauce). Stir in the mustard, lemon juice, capers, parsley and crème fraîche and taste for seasoning.

Melt the rest of the butter in a frying pan and gently sauté the leeks for three minutes. Splash in 2 tbsp of water, season, cover and cook over a low heat until tender, about seven minutes. If there are lots of juices, increase the heat to reduce them.

Add the chicken to the sauce, then bring to the boil, reduce the heat and heat the chicken through. Gently stir in the leeks and taste. You may want to add more lemon juice or mustard. Put the mixture into a 25 x 20cm (10 x 8in) pie dish – I like an enamel one as it conducts the heat well – and leave to cool.

Preheat the oven to 200°C/400°F/gas mark 6. On a lightly floured surface, roll the pastry out to the thickness of a 50 pence coin. Cut off a strip the same width as the lip of the pie dish. Wet the lip and press this strip on to it. Brush the strip with water and lay the rest of the pastry on top. Press the pastry lid on to the pastry strip, then cut off the excess. Crimp the edges and use the remaining pastry to decorate the top of the pie.

Make three small slits in the pastry (near the middle) to let the steam escape. Brush the top with the egg mixture and put into the oven for 30–40 minutes, or until the pastry is a deep golden colour and puffed up. Serve immediately.

chicken, leek and cider pie with mature cheddar and hazelnut crumble

The most old-fashioned dish in the book and one of my family's favourites. I can turn out meals that come from the Lebanon, Turkey and Brazil – full of interesting ingredients and exotic flavours – but they still ask for this. It needs good seasoning, so pay attention to that bit.

SERVES 6

FOR THE FILLING

400g (14oz) leeks
40g (1½oz) unsalted butter
200ml (7fl oz) cider
50g (1¾oz) plain flour
300ml (½ pint) whole milk
salt and pepper
1½ tsp Dijon mustard
400g (14oz) cooked chicken,
  torn into pieces
2 tbsp double cream (optional)

FOR THE CRUMBLE

100g (3½oz) plain flour
100g (3½oz) breadcrumbs
125g (4½oz) cold unsalted
  butter, cut into small cubes
35g (1¼oz) hazelnuts, roughly
  chopped
60g (2oz) mature Cheddar,
  grated
30g (1oz) Parmesan, grated
1 tbsp finely chopped parsley
  leaves

Preheat the oven to 190°C/375°F/gas mark 5. Remove the discoloured outer leaves from the leeks and trim the dark tops and bases. Cut the leeks into 2.5cm (1in) lengths and wash thoroughly under running water; you need to remove any trapped soil.

Melt 15g (½oz) of the butter in heavy-based saucepan and add the leeks. Cook over a medium heat for about five minutes, they shouldn't become coloured. Add 2 tbsp of the cider and cover the pan. Cook on a low heat for another five to seven minutes. The leeks should become soft, but retain their shape.

Meanwhile, melt the rest of the butter in a separate saucepan and add the flour. Stir the flour into the butter and cook it over a medium heat for about a minute. Take the pan off the heat and add the milk a little at a time, stirring well after each addition to incorporate the liquid into the roux and keep the mixture smooth. After you've added all the milk add the remaining cider, too. Return the saucepan to the heat and bring to the boil, stirring all the time, to form a thick sauce. Reduce the heat and simmer for three minutes to 'cook out' the flour. Season, add the mustard, then stir in the leeks (with their cooking juices) and the chicken. Heat all this through thoroughly, add the cream if you're using it (it brings a touch of luxury but isn't necessary) and taste for seasoning. Pour the mixture into an ovenproof pie dish.

To make the crumble, put the flour, breadcrumbs and butter into a bowl and rub the mixture between your fingers until little lumps have formed. Add the rest of the crumble ingredients and season well. Spread this over the top of the filling and cook in the hot oven for 30 minutes, until the top is golden brown. Serve immediately. I like a watercress salad on the side and a few boiled waxy potatoes.

chicken, corn and potato soup with spicy avocado and lime salsa

A real meal in a bowl and a good way to use home-made stock and leftover chicken. If you have more chicken than suggested in the recipe just bung it all in, though you do need to use more stock or you'll have a very thick potful.

If you don't want to go to the trouble of making the salsa, serve with a splash of chilli sauce, a squeeze of lime and a handful of chopped coriander.

SERVES 4

FOR THE SOUP

1 tbsp olive oil
10g (¼oz) unsalted butter
1 onion, roughly chopped
1 large leek, roughly chopped
1 tbsp ground cumin
½ tbsp ground coriander
300g (10½oz) potato, peeled and chopped
salt and pepper
800ml (1 pint 7fl oz) chicken stock
75g (2¾oz) crème fraîche
160g (5¾oz) sweetcorn
125–150g (4½–5½oz) cooked chicken, torn into pieces

FOR THE SALSA

250g (9oz) tomatoes
2 garlic cloves
2 spring onions
3 red chillies, deseeded
2 avocados, roughly chopped
1½ tsp ground cumin
juice of ½ lime
4 tbsp chopped coriander
4 tbsp extra virgin olive oil

To make the soup, heat the olive oil and butter in a large saucepan and sauté the onion and leek over a medium heat for a couple of minutes. Add the spices and stir them around while they release their flavour. Now put in the potatoes and make sure they get a good coating in the fat and cooking juices. Season. Cover the pan, reduce the heat to low and let the vegetables sweat for 20 minutes. Check every so often to make sure that the mixture is not in danger of boiling dry; add half a wine glass of water if it needs more moisture.

Pour the chicken stock on to the vegetables, season and simmer for a further 10 minutes. Stir in the crème fraîche and add the sweetcorn and chicken. Add more stock or water if the mixture is too thick. Heat through thoroughly, then check the seasoning.

Meanwhile, make the salsa as on page 82. It will keep for a couple of hours without spoiling.

Serve the soup with a spoonful of salsa on top.

freekeh with chilli-fried chicken, cumin and coriander-roast winter vegetables, tahini dressing

A healthy, earthy, Middle Eastern-inspired ensemble. I do make it with leftovers (it makes a little go a long way) but you can also cook chicken especially for it – use skinless boneless thighs – as it's a good party or lunch dish. Offer a bowl of yogurt flavoured with garlic on the side, and shreds of preserved lemon skin as well, as it's good contrasted with sharp, bright flavours.

SERVES 4–6

FOR THE DRESSING

200ml (7fl oz) tahini

5 tbsp extra virgin olive oil

juice of ½ lemon, or to taste

salt and pepper

2 tsp sherry vinegar

2 garlic cloves, crushed

FOR THE DISH

1 medium cauliflower

½ tbsp coriander seeds, toasted
   and crushed (see page 66)

¼ tsp chilli flakes

extra virgin olive oil

8–12 slim carrots

2 tsp cumin seeds

finely grated zest of 1 orange,
   plus 2 tbsp orange juice

200g (7oz) freekeh

juice of ½ lemon

1 tbsp olive oil

1 large onion, finely sliced

300g (10½oz) cooked chicken,
   torn into pieces

2 tbsp roughly chopped
   coriander leaves

2 tbsp roughly chopped
   flat-leaf parsley leaves

about ¼ tsp sumac

Preheat the oven to 180°C/350°F/gas mark 4. To make the dressing, just whisk all the ingredients together in a jug, using a fork, with 75ml (2½fl oz) of warm water. Different brands of tahini vary in thickness, so you may need to add more water accordingly, then adjust the seasoning (and that means lemon juice as well as salt and pepper) to taste. Just as with a vinaigrette, you have to taste a tahini dressing as you go along to make sure you're happy with it.

Break the cauliflower into florets and put them into a roasting tin. Sprinkle with the crushed coriander seeds, chilli flakes, salt and pepper. Drizzle with 2 tbsp of virgin oil and turn the cauliflower over with your hands to make sure it all gets coated. Wash the carrots thoroughly. If they're young and I've been able to clean them well, I tend not to peel them. Put these into another small roasting tin and add the cumin seeds, 1 tbsp more virgin oil, seasoning and the orange zest and juice. Toss with your hands to mix. Put the vegetables in the hot oven and cook for 30 minutes, turning them halfway through.

Meanwhile, cook the freekeh. Put it into a saucepan and cover with water. Bring to the boil, then reduce the heat and cook for 20–25 minutes, or until tender. Drain and toss with seasoning, 4 tbsp of virgin oil and the lemon juice.

Heat the 1 tbsp of regular oil in a frying pan and sauté the onion until golden brown. Add the chicken and cook until it is thoroughly hot. Season.

Toss the freekeh with the chicken, onions, herbs and the roasted vegetables, being really careful not to break up the vegetables. Serve on a heated platter or broad shallow bowl. Drizzle the tahini dressing over the top (offer the rest in a bowl) and sprinkle on the sumac. Serve immediately.

down to the bones: perfect stock

Sometimes I think we have the wrong focus. Much of the excitement surrounding food nowadays is to do with new wonder ingredients and the thrill (and convenience) of quick cooking. I'm guilty of this myself. We're all very focused on 'the look', too: a beautifully arranged plate, a torrent of colour.

But in cooking it is important to go back, too, I mean back to the fundamentals. You are never going to carry a pot of broth to the table with a self-congratulatory 'Ta-dah!' but you should. Just as it's satisfying to use up leftovers, it's important to get right down to the bones, to drag flavour – and goodness – out of a chicken carcass or a bag of wings you've bought for a song.

I know it's easy to buy fresh stock. It's not bad if you're desperate, but it bears no resemblance to home-made… and just look at the price! The ingredients for stock are so simple, the hands-on attention so minimal – you just leave it to bubble soothingly – that tipping a chicken carcass into the bin seems, somehow, wrong. And it isn't just a matter of frugality; the smell of stock as it cooks is restorative. It's an old-fashioned smell which spells care and comfort. And the flavour of a well-made stock – savoury and sweet, herbal and deep – seems to go on and on, to somehow get into your core.

I make two different kinds of stock, the old-fashioned type I grew up with and a gently spiced pot of Eastern goodness. For both you can use either cooked bones or raw. For regular stock, put the bones in a large pot with two celery sticks, eight black peppercorns, a couple of bay leaves, a peeled and halved onion, a large carrot and a handful of parsley stalks. Even if you're using a cooked carcass, throw in a few raw chicken wings too, they really help. You should never add salt, as reduced stock is salty. And don't add tomatoes, as the seeds can impart bitterness. Cover with a couple of litres of water, slowly bring to the boil, skim and reduce the heat to a gentle simmer. Cook for two hours, skimming frequently, then strain. Never allow the stock to boil as it muddies the flavour and makes it cloudy. You want a clear golden broth.

For an Eastern stock – to use in broths and South East Asian braises or sautés – I put onion, peeled garlic and a generous chunk of chopped root ginger into the pot, then other aromatics, depending on what the stock will be used for. It could be lemon grass and lime leaves with coriander, a bit of star anise, chilli or strips of lime zest. I cook this stock in exactly the same way as the more familiar type.

With stock in your fridge or freezer, you have a basic block on which to build a meal. You have a store of condensed flavour, ready to be tapped. I've said it's an old-fashioned smell but I don't want it to become the smell of the past. I would like the scent of stock cooking to be a modern smell, too. It's good to get right down to the bones.

bird in a broth

Chicken stock isn't just to make soups or risottos. It can become the core of a meal, a foundation to build on. Think of an old-fashioned broth, but more exotic (and more substantial) and you've got the idea. The broth-based dishes on the next few pages are among my favourites. The Asian versions are head-clearing; the Middle Eastern one – thick with freekeh, herbs and olive oil – is restorative. I could have gone on in this vein, but I'll leave that up to you. You have a big pot of stock. Cook some orzo in it and add scraps of chicken, lemon and lots of dill, or pumpkin, beans and shavings of Parmesan, or fill it with layers of chicken, kale, crumbled bread or cooked rice and big handfuls of grated Gruyère. A saucepan of stock, with the bits and pieces of meat you've rescued from your roast, are the beginnings of another good meal.

chicken and freekeh broth with herbs

A Middle Eastern-inspired broth, simple and clean-tasting. You can use pearl barley, farro or spelt instead of the freekeh, each one will just change the feel of it slightly. (Just make sure you know the cooking times.) Every bowlful of soup is made by the eater, the embellishments added according to taste. If you're craving heat, a teaspoonful of harissa paste in each serving is good, too.

SERVES 6

2 tbsp extra virgin olive oil,
plus more to serve
4 shallots, sliced
3 garlic cloves, sliced
1.4 litres (2½ pints) chicken
stock
100g (3½oz) freekeh
1 small fennel bulb
juice of ½ lemon, plus lemon
wedges to serve
200g (7oz) cooked chicken,
torn into pieces
leaves from 6 sprigs of mint,
plus more to serve
3 tbsp chopped flat-leaf
parsley, plus more to serve
2 tbsp each chopped dill and
coriander, plus more to serve

Heat the oil in a medium-large saucepan and gently sauté the shallots until soft but not coloured. Add the garlic and cook for another couple of minutes. Pour on the stock, reduce the heat to a simmer, then tip in the freekeh.

Halve the fennel, remove the coarse outer leaves, then trim the top, reserving any little fronds. Trim the base, but not too much or the halved bulb could fall apart. Cut each half into wafer-thin slices – a mandoline is the best tool for this – and squeeze lemon over them.

When the freekeh is tender – it takes 20–25 minutes – add the fennel and the chicken and cook for couple of minutes, then add the herbs. Check for seasoning, add a good slug of extra virgin olive oil and serve with a bowl of Greek yogurt with crushed garlic and lemon wedges, more herbs and olive oil.

ginger-chicken meatballs in broth with greens

This is a good supper: uplifting, light, energizing and head-clearing. Add other vegetables – spinach, broccoli, thin slices of mushroom, edamame beans – to the pak choi, or use them instead of it. Minced turkey also works if you can't get minced chicken. And yes, minced chicken is not leftovers, I do realize that. But this dish earns its place in this chapter because it uses stock, made from the remains of your Sunday roast.

SERVES 4

500g (1lb 2oz) minced chicken
2 garlic cloves, finely grated
1 tbsp soy sauce
2cm (¾in) root ginger, peeled and finely grated, plus 2 slices, each the thickness of a pound coin
4 spring onions, finely chopped
salt and pepper
1.2 litres (2 pints) chicken stock
1 red chilli, halved, deseeded and finely chopped, plus more to serve (optional)
2 tbsp rapeseed or groundnut oil, or any other oil you prefer
2 heads of pak choi, leaves separated and halved lengthways
juice of 1 lime

Using your hands, mix together the chicken, garlic, soy sauce, grated ginger and half the spring onions. Season. Wet your hands and shape the mixture into little balls each about the size of a walnut in its shell. If you have time to chill these, so much the better as they'll be easier to work with. Put them on a baking sheet, cover with cling film and put in the fridge for 30 minutes.

Bring the chicken stock to the boil and add the slices of ginger and half the chilli. Reduce the heat to low and simmer for 10 minutes. Take off the heat (this is just to flavour the broth with ginger).

Heat the oil in a medium-large frying pan and cook the meatballs in two batches, turning them over to make sure they get colour all over. It will take about 10 minutes. Transfer to a plate using a slotted spoon. If there is any fat in the pan, pour it out, but don't wash the pan.

Add the stock to the pan and bring to the boil, scraping the base of the pan with a wooden spoon. Reduce the heat, return the meatballs, then bring to a simmer and cook for three minutes. Add the bok choi and the rest of the chilli and cook for another three minutes. The meatballs should be cooked through and the bok choi tender. Fish out the slices of ginger. Add the lime juice and remaining spring onions, taste for seasoning and serve, sprinkled with more chilli if you like.

vietnamese chicken pho

In Vietnam this is made with freshly cooked chicken – the aromatics added as the chicken simmers – but I make it with stock (flavouring it with aromatics) and add leftover chicken. It's a brilliant way to make the best of a small amount of meat. Everything depends on the broth, which should be golden and fragrant; a rich stock, made with a carcass and the addition of chicken wings, is especially good (see page 216).

The embellishments – the herbs, shallots, chillies and beansprouts – should be added by diners at the table and you should offer wedges of lime, too, so people can season their pho to taste. That way, everything stays fresh and crisp. Offer Asian chilli sauce, such as sriracha, for people to add if they want. The noodles can be cooked in the soup, but they make it cloudy which spoils the sense of freshness.

SERVES 4–6

FOR THE PHO

1.2 litres (2 pints) chicken stock

4 thin slices of root ginger

½ star anise

2 garlic cloves, sliced

1 red chilli, deseeded and finely sliced

125g (4½oz) dried rice noodles

250ml (9fl oz) groundnut oil

4 banana shallots, or 7 regular shallots, peeled and sliced

salt

4 tbsp fish sauce

juice of 1 lime

2 tsp caster sugar

200g (7oz) cooked chicken, torn into pieces

TO SERVE

leaves from a bunch of Thai basil (or regular basil), torn

leaves from a bunch of coriander

4 spring onions, chopped

100g (3½oz) beansprouts

lime wedges

2 red chillies, deseeded and finely sliced

Put the stock into a saucepan. Add the ginger, star anise, garlic and chilli. Bring to the boil, reduce the heat and simmer gently for about 15 minutes. Scoop out the ginger and star anise.

Prepare the noodles according to the instructions on the packet.

Now for the crispy shallots. Heat the oil in a small saucepan over a medium heat until it reaches 135°C (275°F) on a kitchen thermometer. Add the shallots and cook, stirring frequently, otherwise they will cook unevenly, until golden. It will take about six minutes. Scoop them up with a slotted spoon and put them on a double thickness of absorbent kitchen paper.

Set a heatproof bowl on a work surface and put a metal sieve (not a plastic one) on top of it (you will drain the shallots and oil in this after another frying). Increase the heat under the oil and, once it registers 190°C (375°F) on the thermometer, return the shallots and cook until they are crispy and well-browned. This happens quickly, so you have to work fast. Quickly and carefully pour the oil and shallots through the sieve to stop the shallots cooking, then transfer the shallots to a double thickness of kitchen paper. Leave so the paper can soak up the excess oil. Sprinkle with salt. You can keep these, stored in an airtight container, for two days, although they're really better fresh.

Add the fish sauce, lime juice and sugar to the broth and heat it, then add the chicken and warm through. Put the broth into bowls, adding some noodles, and serve. You should have the herbs, spring onions, beansprouts, lime wedges, chillies and crispy shallots on the table, ready for diners to finish off their own bowls as they like.

index

Baked chicken with tarragon and Dijon mustard 15

Balinese chicken, bean and coconut salad 112

Barbecued poussins with za'atar and roast pumpkin
houmous 160

Bird pie 210

Bollito misto 142

booze and chicken 30

Bourbon and marmalade-glazed drumsticks 27

braising chicken 42–3

Brazilian chicken and prawn xinim 70

Buttermilk chicken with chipotle slaw 168

Caramelized ginger chicken, Vietnamese 68

Casa Lucio's chicken with garlic 29

Cavatelli with chicken, pancetta, peas and cream
209

Cherry and bulgar-stuffed poussins in vine leaves
94

Chicken, corn and potato soup with spicy avocado
and lime salsa 213

Chicken and freekeh broth with herbs 217

Chicken and peanut stew, West African 64

Chicken and prawn xinxim, Brazilian 70

Chicken and pumpkin laksa 202

Chicken and pumpkin with pepita pesto,
Mexican 12

Chicken and rice, Puerto Rican 25

Chicken and spinach meatballs with tomato
sauce 181

Chicken and sweet potato curry, Vietnamese 204

Chicken, asparagus, broad bean and radish salad 128

Chicken, bacon and potato salad with buttermilk
and herb dressing 131

Chicken, bean and coconut salad, Balinese 112

Chicken braised with shallots and chicory on
Jerusalem artichoke purée 96

Chicken breasts with wild mushroom sauce and Puy
lentils 98

Chicken burgers with Asian slaw, Thai 20

Chicken curry, Kachin 24

Chicken curry with love apples and rum,
Jamaican 53

Chicken, date and lentil brown rice pilaf 206

Chicken fatteh 153

Chicken, fennel and pancetta gratin 205

Chicken forestière 44

Chicken in bitter orange and guava adobo 69

Chicken in the pot with vegetables and barley 197

Chicken, leek and cider pie with mature cheddar
and hazelnut crumble 212

Chicken, leek and pea speltotto with vermouth 208

Chicken legs in pinot noir with sour cherries and
parsnip purée 84

Chicken Messina 113

Chicken, morcilla and sherry 10

Chicken Orvieto 81

Chicken pho, Vietnamese 220

Chicken piri piri 156

Chicken pot-roasted in milk, bay and nutmeg
186

Chicken rice, Hainan 57

Chicken rye schnitzel with mustard sauce 38

Chicken, Serrano ham and sherried pear salad with
quince dressing 127

Chicken shish with toum 159

Chicken, soft spring onions and baby potatoes 41

Chicken, spinach and cauliflower risotto with
melting fontina 199

chicken stock 216

Chicken stuffed with courgettes and ricotta 97

chicken thighs 170

Chicken with anchovies, lemon and rosemary 36

Chicken with apricots, Parsee 66

Chicken with dill and leeks 176

Chicken with garlic, Casa Lucio's 29

Chicken with greens, capers and skordalia,
Greek 141

Chicken with griddled leeks, roast peppers and
salbitxada 158

Chicken with leeks, apples and cider 192

Chicken with marsala, olives and blood oranges 34

Chicken with pistachios and mint, Persian 104

Chicken with prunes in red wine 19

Chicken with pumpkin, cream and Gruyère 180

Chicken with rice, sweet potato and pepper stuffing, coriander and coconut sauce 65

Chicken with Riesling, leeks and grapes 47

Chicken with Shaoxing wine, crisp radishes and pickled ginger 40

Chicken with spring vegetables and herbed cream 77

Chicken with thyme and lemon and smashed garlic potatoes 185

Chicken with tzimmes, Jewish 151

Chicken with *vin jaune* and morels, Jura 140

Cider-brined chicken with prunes, chestnuts and baby onions 135–6

citrus fruits and chicken 116

Coriander seared chicken with hot-and-cold cucumber relish 171

Coronation chicken, mango and avocado 124

cream/crème fraîche and chicken 178

Crusted chicken and chorizo paella 138

Cumin and lime-scented potato salad with date and tamarind chutney 52

Cumin and turmeric roast chicken with smashed avocado and corn cakes 16

Freekeh with chilli-fried chicken, cumin and coriander-roast winter vegetables, tahini dressing 215

Fried chicken wings, Korean 62

fruit and chicken 190

Ginger beer can chicken 163

Ginger-chicken meatballs in broth with greens 218

Greek chicken with greens, capers and skordalia 141

Griddled chicken, sweet potato and avocado salad with chipotle mayo, Mexican 130

Griddled chicken with smoky chilli butter 167

Guisado de pollo 60

Hainan chicken rice 57

herbs and chicken 102

Hot and sweet lime chicken wings 189

Hot Italian chicken with peppers and chilli 28

Indian-spiced chicken with coriander chutney 166

Indonesian roast spiced chicken with mango and tomato salad 61

Jamaican chicken curry with love apples and rum 53

Jerusalem artichokes and chicken with anchovy, walnut and parsley relish 37

Jewish chicken with tzimmes 151

Jura chicken with *vin jaune* and morels 140

Kachin chicken curry 24

Korean chicken wings 62

Lemon and pistachio chicken 92

Lemon grass and chilli chicken, Vietnamese 22

Lemon grass and turmeric chicken with potato salad, Roopa's 50

Mar i muntanya 144

Mexican chicken and pumpkin with pepita pesto 12

Mexican griddled chicken, sweet potato and avocado salad with chipotle mayo 130

Middle Eastern rose-scented poussins with sour cherries and yogurt 145

Mustard chicken, black beans and avocado salsa 82

Negima yakitori 172

Palm sugar-griddled chicken with radishes, cucumber and rice vermicelli 118

Paprika roast chicken with caraway potatoes, quick-pickled cucumber and soured cream 87

Parsee chicken with apricots 66

Persian chicken with pistachios and mint 104

Pollo cubano with fried eggs and plantains 54

Pomegranate and honey-glazed chicken
    skewers 165
Pot-roast chicken with bacon, baby gems and
    creamy parsley sauce 198
Pot-roast chicken with figs 194
Poule au pot with caper and shallot cream 195
Poulet au vinaigre 100
Poulet bonne femme 46
Poussins with black grapes, juniper and saba
    78
Poussins with Indian spices and fresh coriander
    and coconut chutney 80
Puerto Rican chicken and rice 25

Roast chicken and pumpkin, black lentils and
    hazelnut picada 107
Roast chicken, garlic and potatoes in the pan with
    watercress, Cashel Blue and walnut butter 21
Roast chicken stuffed with black pudding and apple,
    mustard sauce 93
Roast chicken with mushroom and sage butter
    under the skin 101
Roast chicken with peaches, honey and
    lavender 74
Roast chicken with truffles 150
Roast spiced chicken with mango and tomato salad,
    Indonesian 61
roasting chickens 88–9
Roopa's lemon grass and turmeric chicken with
    potato salad and date and tamarind chutney 50
Rose-scented poussins with sour cherry sauce,
    Middle Eastern 145
Royal chicken korma 146

Salad of chicken, cherries and watercress with
    creamy tarragon dressing 110
Salad of Japanese griddled thighs with edamame,
    sugar snaps and miso dressing 126
Saltimbocca 14
sautéing chicken 42, 43
Smoked chicken, lentil and sautéed Jerusalem
    artichoke salad 120

Smoked paprika roast chicken, potato wedges and
    saffron allioli 149
Smoky chicken salad with roast peppers, shiitake
    and sugar snap peas 123
Soothing North Indian chicken 183
Spiced roast chicken with barley-pomegranate
    stuffing and Georgian aubergine pkhali 91

Tajine of chicken, caramelized onions and pears 58
Thai chicken burgers with Asian slaw 20
Thyme-roasted chicken with Breton onion sauce 182
Turkish-spiced chicken with hot green relish 32

Vietnamese caramelized ginger chicken 68
Vietnamese chicken and sweet potato curry 204
Vietnamese chicken pho 220
Vietnamese lemon grass and chilli chicken 22

Warm salad of chipotle-griddled chicken, chorizo
    and quinoa with lime crème fraîche 114
Warm salad of griddled chicken, freekeh, preserved
    lemon, sour cherries and mint 121
West African chicken and peanut stew 64

all eggs used in the book are large unless
otherwise stated

for hard-to-find food items used in the book,
please try the following online suppliers:
www.coolchile.co.uk
www.melburyandappleton.com
www.seasonedpioneers.com
www.souschef.co.uk

For Martha Munro, an outstanding teacher who made a huge difference to my life

acknowledgements

There are some great recipes in this book and not all of them are mine. They're all credited (in the right places), but I would especially like to thank Roopa Gulati for the wonderful lemon grass and turmeric chicken recipe and for guiding me through the perfect chicken korma. I seem to end up with at least one of Roopa's dishes in every book (once she starts describing something she's cooked, she has me begging for the recipe). Thanks, R. Never stop cooking. Or enthusing...

Thanks also to Faith Durand who seduced me into trying chicken cooked in milk (and it is lovely) on her website www.kitchn.com; to Helen and Hannah Toeman who helped me with background on Jewish cooking (especially chicken) and to lovely Bonnie Benwick, food writer for the *Washington Post*, who gave me masterful instructions on how to make the Lebanese garlic paste, toum. Garlic and schmaltz kisses to all of you.

My colleague Bee Wilson is always the first person I turn to for help with matters historical and she never lets me down. Nobody knows as much about food history as she does. Thank you, Bee.

On shoots, assistants Rachel Wood, Kathryn Bruton and Emma Godwin were total troopers who threw themselves into the fray. We could never have produced so many dishes without you all.

Back at Octopus HQ, publishing director Denise Bates gave advice when we needed it and let us have space when we didn't: the best kind of publisher you could have. Thanks too to Jonathan Christie, Sybella Stephens, Katherine Hockley and Fran Johnson for overseeing design and all the various processes that a book goes through and to Kevin Hawkins and Terry Shaughnessy for doing the most important business (selling it).

Dear Ben, Ted and Gillies, you ate more chicken than is ideal (even if you like chicken). Thanks for staying the course. Maybe one day I will do a dessert book and you'll all be in heaven...

So, to the team: photographer Laura Edwards, editor Lucy Bannell, designer Miranda Harvey and cook Joss Herd. We know each other well, we trust each other, we're prepared to make any kind of suggestion (and nobody will shoot it down). You all give way more than you're paid for – I hope you know I don't take that for granted – and are a joy to work with. (There's nothing better, in my book, than a perfectionist.) If even one of you were missing, the books wouldn't be nearly as good. It's creativity at its very best. Love to you all.